When his people went away Hogg was sent for and he is to be swished to-morrow. We told him he would get it hot and he blubbed.

Sunday—We went for the choir expedition last Thursday. It was great fun. We went to London by the 8.35 train. We missed the train!! So we went by the 8.53. We got to London at 10.15. We then went to the mint we first saw the silver melted and made into thick tablets, then we saw it rolled out into thin bits then cut stamped and weighed then we had a very good luncheon and went to the Tower. We first saw the Bloody Tower were the little Princes were murdered then we saw the jewels the warder said the Queen's crown was worth over £1,000,000 then we saw the armory and the torture's, then we went to Madame Tussaus it is quite a large building now with a large staires then we had tea and went home.

Sunday—I said to Anderson that we might start an aquarium but he said Ferguson had one last term and that it would be copying, he said he hates copying. So we'll have a menagery instead with lizards.

Sunday—The lizard is very well indeed and has eat a lot of worms. White cheeked Jones ma and Mac said they must fight it out in the play-room in the hour. They fought with gloves. White gave him a bloody nose. We had a very good game of football yesterday. Williams and Pierce which left last term came from Eton to play. Pierce changed in my room. He says you don't say squit at Eton and you say Metutors not My tutors. The fireworks are in a week.

Saturday—There was no work this morning as it was "All Saints day." There was a football matsh against another scool—Reynolds'. We won by three goals and three tries.

There was an awful row on Wednesday. Anderson cut off a piece of his hair. Mac nabbed it, and he said he hadn't as he was afraid of the consequenses. Then a search was made and they fond a piece of hair in his drawer. Mac told him he would find himself in Queer Street and Colly said when he was writing home on Sunday that he had better add that he was a liar. Nothing hapened till Monday and Anderson thought it was forgoten but at reading over when the 3nd Div came up the Head said: "Anderson I am astounded at you; you are a shufler and worse." He lost 50 marks and was swished. He would get 20 the head said if he did it again and he would be turned out of the choir.

Sunday—When Colly was out of the room in Set 3 this morning Mason said he wouldn't sneak about me talking if I didn't sneak about him so I talked. When Colly came back Mason sneaked, Please sir will you ask Smith not to talk. I had to stand on the stool of penitence. We are going to put Mason in Coventry because he always sneaks just after he has sworn he won't. Last night we all had to play our pieces in the Drawing Room. I played a duet with Wilson mi. Astley played best. When everybody had played their pieces we had ginger beer and biscuits and went to bed. Fish played worst (on the violin).

Sunday—We had fireworks on the 5th romman candles rockets crackers squibs and a set piece with God Save the Queen on it. They came from Broks who makes the fireworks at the Crystal palace we burnt a man in effigee a man with collars and an axe. The Head said he wouldn't say who it was meant to be but that all true Englishmen who were not traiters could guess. Rowley said it was meant to be Mister Gladstone but he only said this to get a rise out of Pork whose paters a liberal. It was reelly Guy Fawks then Pork said Anderson's father was a liberal too and Anderson hit him in the eye. The Head hates liberals.

There was another row this week; Christy said something to Broadwood at breakfast that the poridge was mighty good. That was copying Anderson who learnt it from his mater who is a Yankee. Mac asked him what he'd said. He said he'd said the porridge was good. Mac asked Is that all you've said. Christy got very red and looked as if he was going to blub and said that was all. Very well said Mac Come afterwards. Mac reported him for telling bungs. He wasn't swished as its his first term: but Mac told him he was making himself very unpopular.

On Tuesday Fatty the butler came into the 3rd Div scoolroom with a message. Some one said in a wisper Hullo Fatty. Mac nabbed it and said who said that nobody answered then Mac said he knew it was Middleton mi as he had recognised his voice Middleton swore he hadn't said a word but he was reported and swished he still swears he didn't say Fatty and I believe it was Pork. The other day at French Campbell went up to Colly and asked him what was wrong with les tables it had a pencil cross on it. Colly said that when he'd corrected it there was no S there. Campbell swore their was. Colly held the paper to the window and said he saw the ink of the S was fresh, then Christy began to blub and said he had done it and Colly said it was a for jerry and wrote forjer in white chalk on his back and said he would tell the chaps in the first Div but he didn't report him to the Head which was awfully decent of him becaus Christy is a new chap.

Sunday—Trials are nearly over. We had Latin G and Greek G paper yesterday (set by the Head). There are only two more papers geography and Latin verse. The Consert is on Saturday. Pork's sister is called Jane!! Campbell saw it on the seel of a letter he got. His people were coming for the Consert but he's written to tell them not to as we told him the Head thought liberals worse than thieves.

CHAPTER II

FROM THE DIARY OF ISEULT OF BRITTANY

May 1—Mamma sent me up a message early this morning to say that I was to put on my best white gown with my coral necklace, as guests were expected. She didn't say who. Nurse was in a fuss and pulled my hair when she did it, and made my face very sore by scrubbing it with pumice-stone. I can't think why, as there was no hurry. I came down punctually at noon. Mamma and papa were sitting in the hall, waiting. Fresh rushes were strewn on the floor. I was told to get out my harp, and to sit with my back to the light. I hadn't practised for weeks, and I can only play one song properly, "The Mallard," a Cornish song. When I told mamma that was the only song I knew, she said I was on no account to mention it, if I was asked to play; but I was only to play Breton songs. I said I didn't know any. She said that didn't matter; but that I could sing anything I knew and call it a Breton song. I said nothing, but I thought, and I still think, this was dishonest. Besides the only songs that I know are quite new. The stable people whistle them, and they come from Rome.

We waited a long time. Papa and mamma were both very fidgety and mamma kept on pulling me about, and telling me that my hair was badly done and that she could see daylight between the pleats of my frock. I nearly cried and papa said: "Leave the dear child alone; she's very good." After we'd been waiting about twenty minutes, the trumpets sounded and Morgan, the seneschal, walked in very slowly, and announced: "Sir Tristram of Lyoness."

Lost Diaries by Maurice Baring

Maurice Baring OBE was born on 27th April 1874 in Mayfair, London. He was the fifth son of eight children to Edward Charles Baring, first Baron Revelstoke, of the Baring banking family, and his wife Louisa Emily Charlotte Bulteel.

After the obligatory years at Eton College he went to Trinity College, Cambridge.

His early career in the diplomatic service was cut short but it gave him a thirst for travel and he did so widely, particularly in Russia. During the Russo-Japanese war of 1904/5 he reported as an eye-witness for the London Morning Post.

In 1909 Baring, who thought of himself as agnostic, converted to Roman Catholicism. A decision which he stated was "the only action in my life which I am quite certain I have never regretted."

When the horror of World War I enveloped Europe in 1914 he enlisted with the Royal Flying Corps, and served as an assistant to David Henderson and Hugh Trenchard (the two responsible for establishing the RFC) on the Western Front in France.

In 1918, Baring served as a staff officer in the Royal Air Force and was appointed Officer of the Order of the British Empire in the 1918 Birthday Honours List.

With the end of the war came his development as a writer. Before the war his works had mainly centrered on journalism, short stories and poetry. Now Baring began to write novels.

In 1925 he gained an honorary commission as a wing commander in the Reserve of Air Force Officers. After his death, Trenchard was to write, "He was the most unselfish man I have ever met or am likely to meet. The Flying Corps owed to this man much more than they know or think."

The last decades of his life proved to be a descent into chronic health problems. For the final 15 years of his life he was debilitated by the increasing onset of Parkinson's Disease.

He was widely known socially, and especially frequented with some of the Cambridge Apostles (an intellectual society at the University founded in 1820), The Coterie (a fashionable group of aristocrats and intellectuals of the 1910s). Baring was staunch in his anti-intellectualism with respect to the arts, and often displayed a lighter side with his pranks on others.

"By all accounts, the real Baring was a charming, affable gentleman who knew how to laugh and had no fear of making a fool of himself."

Maurice Baring, dramatist, poet, novelist, translator, essayist, travel writer and war correspondent, died at Beaufort Castle on 14th December 1945 at the age of 71.

Index of Contents

CHAPTER I

FROM THE DIARY OF SMITH MINOR

ST JAMES'S SCHOOL, September, 1884.

Sunday—Yesterday afternoon was a half-holiday we were playing prisoners base exept four boys who were gardening with Mrs Wickham. Peel hit Bell by mistake with all his force with the pic-axe on Bell's wrist.

Sunday—Last night their was a total eclipse of the moon. We all stayed up to see it, it looked very funny. There was a shadow right over the moon. We began football yesterday. At tea the Head asked if any one had eaten chesnuts in the garden. Simes major said yes at once. Then the Head said he was sure others had too. Then Wilson stood up and after a time 7 chaps stood up. Then the Head said it would be the worse for those who didn't stand up as he knew who the culprets were. I hadn't eaten any but Anderson had given me a piece off his knife so I stood up two. The Head said we should all have two hours extra work. He was very waxy he said we were unreliabel.

Sunday—Yesterday we were all photografed. Simes laughed and was sent to bed for misbehavier. Pork's people came down yesterday. We call Pork Hogg because he's dirty. He showed them over the school, and turned on the electrik light. The Head was looking through the curtain in the library and saw this.

Rather an oldish man walked in, with a reddish beard, and many wrinkles. One of his front teeth was broken and the other was black. He was dressed in a coat of mail which was too tight for him. He had nice eyes and seemed rather embarrassed. Mamma and papa made a great fuss about him and brought me forward and said: "This is our daughter Iseult," and mamma whispered to me: "Show your hands." I didn't want to do this, as nurse had scrubbed them so hard that they were red.

Sir Tristram bowed deeply, and seemed more and more embarrassed. After a long pause he said: "It's a very fine day, isn't it?"

Before I had time to answer, mamma broke in by saying: "Iseult has been up since six with the falconers." This wasn't true and I was surprised that mamma should be so forgetful. I hadn't been out with the hawkers for weeks.

Then dinner was served. It lasted for hours I thought, and the conversation flagged terribly. Kurneval, Sir Tristram's Squire, had twice of everything and drank much more cider than was good for him. After dinner, mamma told me to fetch my harp and to sing a Breton song. I was just going to say I didn't know one, when she frowned at me so severely that I didn't dare. So I sang the Provençal orchard song about waking up too early that Kerodac the groom taught me. Sir Tristram said: "Charming, charming, that's German, isn't it; how well taught she is. I do like good singing." Then he yawned, although he tried not to, and papa said he was sure Sir Tristram was tired, and that he would take him to see the stables. Sir Tristram then became quite lively and said he would be delighted.

When they'd gone, mamma scolded me, and said that I had behaved like a ninny and that she didn't know what our guests would think of me. It seemed to me we only had one guest; but I didn't say so. Then she told me to go and rest so as to be ready for dinner.

I forgot to say that just as Sir Tristram was going out of the room he said to papa: "Your daughter's name is—er?" and papa said, "Yes, Iseult, after her aunt." And Sir Tristram said: "Oh! what a pretty name!"

May 6—They've been here a week now and I haven't seen much of them; because Sir Tristram has been riding with papa nearly all day, and every day. But every day after dinner mamma makes me sing the Provençal song, and every time I sing it, Sir Tristram says: "Charming, charming, that's German, isn't it?" although I've already told him twice now that it isn't. I like Sir Tristram, only he's very silent, and after dinner he becomes sleepy directly, just like papa.

May 7—I've had a most exciting day. Papa and mamma sent for me and when I came into the room they were both very solemn and said they had something particular to say to me. Then mamma cried and papa tried to soothe her and said: "It's all right, it's all right," and then he blurted out that I was to marry Sir Tristram next Wednesday. I cried, and papa cried, and mamma cried, and then they said I was a lucky girl, and mamma said that I must see about my clothes at once.

May 8—Nurse is in a fearful temper. She says we shall never be ready by Wednesday and that it's more than flesh and blood can stand to worrit folks like this. But mamma is in the best of tempers. Sir Tristram has gone away—to stay with some friends—he is coming back on Tuesday night. My wedding gown is to be made of silver with daisies worked on it. The weavers are working day and night, but most of the stuff is old. It belonged to mamma. I do think they might have given me a new gown. Blanche had a new one when she was married.

May 12—The wedding went off very well. I had four maidens and four pages. After Mass, we had a long feast. Papa made a speech and broke down, and Tristram made a speech and got into a muddle about my name, and everybody was silent. Then he said I had beautiful hands and everybody cheered. After supper we were looking out on the sea, and just as Tristram was becoming talkative I noticed that he wore another ring besides his wedding ring, a green one, made of jasper. I said, "What a pretty ring! Who gave it you?" He said, "Oh, a friend," and changed the subject. Then he said he was very tired and went away.

May 13—It's the 13th and that's an unlucky number. Nurse said that no child of hers should marry in May, so I suppose that's what brought it about. In any case Tristram, who has been very gloomy ever since he's been here, has got to go and fight in a tournament. He says he won't be away long and that there's no danger; not any more than crossing the sea in an open boat, which I do think is dangerous. He starts to-morrow at dawn.

May 14—Nothing particular.

May 15—No news.

May 16—Kurneval arrived this evening. He says that Tristram was slightly wounded; but would be all right in a day or two. I am very anxious.

May 17—Tristram was brought back on a litter in the middle of the night. He has been wounded in the arm. The doctors here say he was bandaged wrong by the local doctor. They say he is suffering from slight local pain. Kurneval says the horrid henchman hit his arm as hard as he could with a broad sword. Papa and mamma arrive to-morrow with the doctor. Tristram insists on sleeping out of doors on the beach. The doctor says this is a patient's whim and must be humoured. I'm sure it's bad for him, as the nights are very cold.

July 1—I've been too busy to write my diary for weeks. Tristram is still just the same. The doctors say there is no fear of immediate change.

August 10—Mamma says the Queen of Cornwall (whose name is Iseult the same as mine) is coming for a few days, with her husband and some friends. I do think it's very inconsiderate, considering how full the house is already; and what with Tristram being so ill—and insisting on sleeping on the beach—it makes it very difficult for every one.

September 1—Papa went out to shoot birds with his new cross-bow; but he came back in a bad temper as he'd only shot one, and a hen. Tristram is no better. He keeps on talking about a ship with a black sail.

September 19—To-day I was on the beach with Tristram and he asked me if I saw a ship. I said I did. He asked me if the sail was black, and as the doctor had told me to humour him, I said it was. Upon which he got much worse, and I had to call the doctors. They said he was suffering from hypertrophy of the sensory nerves.

September 20—Tristram unconscious. The Queen of Cornwall just arrived. Too busy to write.

CHAPTER III

FROM THE DIARY OF KING COPHETUA

Cophetua Castle, May 3—We had to be married in May, after all. It was a choice between that and being married on a Friday, and Jane would not hear of that, so I gave in. Poor dear Mamma relented at the end and came to the wedding. On the whole she behaved with great restraint. She could not help saying just a word about rash promises. Jane looked exceedingly beautiful. I felt very proud of her. I regret nothing. We start for Italy to-morrow. We are to visit Milan, Florence-and Rome. Jane is looking forward to the change.

Dijon, May 6—We decided to break the journey here: but we shall probably start again to-morrow, as Jane is extremely dissatisfied with the Inn, the Lion d'Or. I, of course, chose the best. But she says she found a spider in her bedroom; she complained that the silver plates on which dinner was served were not properly cleaned; that the veal was tough, and that we had been given Graves under the guise of Barsac. All these things seem to me exceedingly trivial; but Jane is particular. In a way it is a good thing, but considering her early upbringing and her former circumstances, I confess I am astonished.

Lyons, May 12—I shall be glad when we get to Italy. Jane becomes more and more fastidious about Inns. She walked out of four running, here. I was imprudent enough to say that Mamma had a vassal who was a distant connection of the Sieur Jehan de Blois and Jane insisted on my paying him a visit and asking him to lodge us, telling him who we are, as we are travelling incognito as the Baron and Baroness of Wessex. This put me in a very awkward position, as I don't know him. I did it, however, and Jane came with me. I have seldom felt so awkward, but really he could not have made things easier. He was tact itself, and while respecting our incognito, he treated us with the utmost consideration. He was most kind. Jane made me a little uncomfortable by praising a fine crystal goblet encrusted with emeralds. Sieur Jehan was of course obliged to offer it her, and, to my vexation, she accepted it.

Avignon, May 20—Jane finds our incognito more and more irksome. I was looking forward to a real quiet holiday, where we could get away from all fuss and worry, and all the impediments of rank and riches. I wanted to pretend we were poor for a while. To send on the litters with the oxen, the horses, and the baggage, and to ride on mules—as soon as we had reached the South—but Jane would not hear of this. She said she had had enough of poverty without playing at it now. This is of course quite true, but I wish she wouldn't say such things before people. It makes one so uncomfortable. Here she has insisted on our staying with the Pope, which may put me in a very awkward position with regard to several of our allies in Italy. He has been, however, most gracious. Jane is very impulsive at times. She insisted on our making an expedition to the Bridge here, by moonlight, and dancing on it. She kicked off her shoes and danced barefooted; I asked her not to do this, whereupon she said: "If the courtiers hadn't praised my ankles you would never have married me and what's the use of having pretty ankles, if nobody can see them!" I shall be glad when we get to Italy. I am determined to preserve a strict incognito, once we are across the frontier.

Turin, June 10—It has poured with rain every day since we crossed the frontier, and Jane won't believe that it is ever fine in Italy. It is very cold for the time of year, and the people here say that there has not been such a summer for thirty years. Every time I mention the blue sky of Italy Jane loses her temper. She spends all her time at the goldsmiths' shops and at the weavers'—I am afraid she is extravagant: and her taste in dress is not quite as restrained as I could wish. Of course it doesn't matter here, but at home it would shock people. For instance, last night she came down to supper dressed as a Turkish Sultana in pink trousers and a scimitar, and without even a veil over her face. When I remonstrated she said men did not understand these things.

Milan, June 15—It is still raining. Jane refused to look at the Cathedral and spends her whole time at the merchants' booths as usual. To-day I broached the incognito question. I suggested our walking on foot, or perhaps riding on mules, to Florence. Jane, to my great surprise, said she would be delighted to do this, and asked when we were to start. I said we had better start the day after to-morrow. I am greatly relieved. She is really very sensible, if a little impulsive at times; but considering her early life, it might be much worse. I have much to be thankful for. She is greatly admired, only I wish she would not wear such bright colours.

Florence, June 20—It has been a great disappointment. Just as we were making preparations to start entirely incognito—Jane had even begged that we should walk on foot the whole way and take no clothes with us—a messenger arrived from the Florentine Embassy here, saying that the Duke of Florence had heard of our intended visit and had put a cavalcade of six carriages, fifty mules, seven litters, and a hundred men-at-arms at our disposal. How he could have heard of our intention I don't know! Jane was bitterly disappointed. She cried, and said she had been looking forward to this walking tour more than to anything else. But I managed to soothe her, and she eventually consented to accept the escort of the Duke. It would have been impossible to refuse. As it was, we were very comfortable. We stopped at Bologna on the way, and Jane insisted on going to the market and buying a sausage. She tried to make me taste it, but I cannot endure the taste of garlic.

At Florence we were magnificently received, and taken at once to the Palace—where the rooms are very spacious. Jane complains of the draughts and the cold. It is still pouring with rain. There is a very fine collection of Greek statues to be seen here, but Jane takes no interest in these things. The first thing she did was to go to the New bridge, which is lined with goldsmiths' shops on both sides and to spend a great deal of money on perfectly useless trinkets. She says she must have some things to bring back to my sisters. This was thoughtful of her. The Duke is going to give a great banquet in our honour on Tuesday next.

June 23—The feast is to-night. The gardens have been hung with lanterns: a banquet has been prepared on a gigantic scale. Five hundred guests have been bidden. Jane was greatly looking forward to it and lo and behold! by the most evil mischance a terrible vexation has befallen us. A courier arrived this morning, bearing letters for me, and among them was one announcing the death of the Duke of Burgundy, who is my uncle by marriage. I told Jane that of course we could not possibly be present at the banquet. Jane said that I knew best, but that the Duke would be mortally offended by our absence, since he had arranged the banquet entirely for us and spent a sum of 10,000 ducats on it. It would be, she pointed out—and I am obliged to admit she is right—most impolitic to annoy the Duke. After an hour's reflection I hit on what seemed to me an excellent solution—that we should be present, but dressed in mourning. Jane said this was impossible as she had no black clothes. Then she suggested that I should keep back the news until to-morrow, and if the news were received in other quarters, deny its authenticity, and say we had a later bulletin. This on the whole seemed to be the wisest course. As the etiquette here is very strict and the Dowager Duchess is most particular, I pray that Jane may be careful and guarded in her expressions.

June 25—My poor dear mother was right after all. I should have listened, and now it is too late. The dinner went off very well. We sat at a small table on a raised dais. Jane sat between the Duke and the Prime Minister and opposite the Dowager Duchess. There was no one at the table, except myself, under sixty years of age, and only the greatest magnates were present. Jane was silent and demure and becomingly dressed. I congratulated myself on everything. After the banquet came the dance, and Jane took part with exquisite grace in the saraband: she observed all the rules of etiquette. The Dowager Duchess seemed charmed with her. Then later came supper, which was served in a tent, and which was perhaps more solemn than everything. When the time came to lead Jane to supper she was nowhere to be found. Outside in the garden the minor nobles were dancing in masks, and some mimes were singing. We waited, and then a message came that the Queen had had a touch of ague and had retired. The supper went off gloomily. At the close an enormous pie was brought in, the sight of which caused a ripple of well-bred applause. "Viva Il Re Cophetua" was written on it in letters of pink sugar. It was truly a triumph of culinary art. The mime announced that the moment had come for it to be cut, and as the Grand Duke rose to do this the thin crust burst of itself, and out stepped Jane, with no garments beside her glorious dark hair! She tripped on to the table, and then with a peal of laughter leapt from it and ran into the garden, since when she has not been heard of! My anguish and shame are too great for words.

But the Duke and the Dowager have been most sympathetic.

June 26—Jane has fled, and my jewels as well as hers are missing.

It is suspected that the attaché at the Florentine Embassy at Milan is at the bottom of the conspiracy, for Jane herself had a good heart.

CHAPTER IV

FROM THE DIARY OF FROISSART, WAR CORRESPONDENT

Parys, The Feast of the Epiphanie—The astrologers say there will be plenty-full trouble in Normandy, in the spring.

June 10—To dyner with the Cardinall of Piergourt to meet the gentyll King of Behayne and the Lorde Charles, his son. The Cardinall sayd neither the Kynge of Englande nor the Frenche Kynge desire warre, but the honour of them and of their people saved, they wolde gladly fall to any reasonable way. But the King of Behayne shook his heade and sayd: "I am feare I am a pesymyste," which is Almayne for a man who beholds the future with no gladde chere.

June 20—The great merchaunt of Araby, Montefior, says there will be no warre. He has received worde from the cytie of London, and his friends, great merchaunts all, and notably, Salmone and Glukstyn, sayd likewise that there will be no warre.

June 30—The currours have brought worde home, the Kynge of Englande was on the see with a great army, and is now a lande in Normandy. Have received faire offers for chronycles of the warre from London, Parys, and Rome; they offer three thousand crounes monthly, payeing curtesly for all my expenses. Have sayd I will gladly fall to their wish.

July 1—Trussed bagge and baggage in great hast and departed towarde Normandy, the seat of warre.

July 2—Ryde but small journeys, and do purpose, being no great horseman, every time I have to ryde a horse, to add three crounes to the expenses which my patrons curtesly pay.

Take lodgynges every day bytwene noone and thre of the clocke. Finde the contrey frutefull and reasonably suffycent of wyne.

July 3, Cane—A great and ryche town with many burgesses, crafty men. They solde wyne so deare that there were no byers save myself who bought suffycent and added to the lyste which my patrons curtesly pay.

July 4, Amyense—Left Cane and the englysshmen have taken the toune and clene robbed it. Right pensyve as to putting my lyfe in adventure.

Sir Godmar de Fay is to kepe note of the chronyclers and he has ordayned them to bring him their chronycles. He has curtesly made these rules for the chronyclers. Chronyclers may only chronycle the truth. Chronyclers may not chronycle the names of places, bridges, rivers, castels where batayles happen—nor the names of any lordes, knyghtes, marshals, erles, or others who take part in the batayle: nor the names of any weapons or artillery used, nor the names or numbers of any prisoners taken in batayle.

Thanks to Sir Godmar de Fay the chronycler's task has been made lyghter.

July 6, Calys—The chronyclers have been ordayned by Sir Godmar de Fay to go to Calys. There are nine chronyclers. One is an Alleymayne, who is learned in the art of warre, one is a Genowayes, and one an Englysshman, the rest are Frenche. The cytie of Calys is full of drapery and other merchauntdyse, noble ladyes and damosels. The chronyclers have good wyl to stay in the cytie.

July 7—Sir Godmar de Fay has ordayned all the chronyclers to leave the cytie of Calys and to ride to a lytell town called Nully, where there are no merchauntdyse, and no damosels, nor suffycent of wyne. The chronyclers are not so merrie as in the cytie of Calys.

July 9—Played chesse with the Genowayse and was checkmate with a bishop.

August 6—The chronyclers are all pensyve. They are lodged in the feldes. There has fallen a great rayne that pours downe on our tents. There is no wyne nor pasties, nor suffycent of flesshe, no bookes for to rede, nor any company.

Last nyghte I wrote a ballade on Warre, which ends, "But Johnnie Froissart wisheth he were dead." It is too indiscrete to publysh. I wysh I were at Calys. I wysh I were at Parys. I wysh I were anywhere but at Nully.

August 23—At the Kynge's commandment the chronyclers are to go to the fronte.

August 25, Friday—The Kynge of Englande and the French Kynge have ordayned all the business of a batayle. I shall watch it and chronycle it from a hill, which shall not be too farre away to see and not too neare to adventure my lyfe.

August 26—I rode to a windmill but mistooke the way, as a great rayne fell, then the eyre waxed clere and I saw a great many Englyssh erls and Frenche knyghtes, riding in contrarie directions, in hast. Then many Genowayse went by, and the Englysshmen began to shote feersly with their crossbowes and their arowes fell so hotly that I rode to a lytell hut, and finding shelter there I wayted till the snowe of arowes should have passed. Then I clymbed to the top of the hill but I could see lytell but dyverse men riding here and there. When I went out again, aboute evensong, I could see no one aboute, dyverse knyghtes and squyers rode by looking for their maisters, and then it was sayd the Kynge had fought a batayle, and had rode to the castell of Broye, and thence to Amyense.

August 30—The chronyclers have been ordayned to go to Calys, whereat they are well pleased save for a feare of a siege. The chronyclers have writ the chronicle of the Day of Saturday, August 26. It was a great batayle, ryght cruell, and it is named the batayle of Cressey.

Some of the chronyclers say the Englysshmen discomfyted the French; others that the King discomfyted the Englysshe; but the Englysshmen repute themselves to have the victorie; but all this shall be told in my chronicle, which I shall write when I am once more in the fayre cytie of Parys. It was a great batayle and the Frenche and the Englysshe Lordes are both well pleased at the feats of arms, and the Frenche Kynge, though the day was not as he wolde have had it, has wonne hygh renowne and is ryght pleased—likewise the Englysshe Kynge, and his son; but both Kynges have ordayned the chronyclers to make no boast of their good adventure.

August 30—The Kynge of Englande has layd siege to Calys and has sayd he will take the towne by famysshing. When worde of this was brought to the chronyclers they were displeased. It is well that I have hyd in a safe place some wyne and other thynges necessarie.

Later—All thynges to eat are solde at a great pryce. A mouse costs a croune.

August 31—All the poore and mean people were constrained by the capture of Calys to yssue out of the town, men, women, and children, and to pass through the Englysshe host, and with them the poore chronyclers. And the Kynge of Englande gave them and the chronyclers mete and drinke to dyner, and every person ii d. sterlying in alms.

And the chronyclers have added to the lyst of their costs which their patrons curtesly pay: To loss of honour at receiving alms from an Englysshe Kynge, a thousand crounes.

CHAPTER V

FROM THE DIARY OF GEORGE WASHINGTON WRITTEN WHEN A SCHOOLBOY

Bridges Creek, 1744, September 20—My mother has at last consented to let me go to school. I had repeatedly made it quite plain to her that the private tuition hitherto accorded to me was inadequate; that I would be in danger of being outstripped in the race owing to insufficient groundwork. My mother, although very shrewd in some matters, was curiously obstinate on this point. She positively declined to let me attend the day-school, saying that she thought I knew quite enough for a boy of my age, and that it would be time enough for me to go to school when I was older. I quoted to her Tacitus' powerful phrase about the insidious danger of indolence; how there is a charm in indolence—but let me taste the full pleasure of transcribing the noble original: "Subit quippe etiam ipsius inertiæ dulcedo: et invisa primo desidia postremo amatur"; but she only said that she did not understand Latin. This was scarcely an argument, as I translated it for her.

I cannot help thinking that there was sometimes an element of pose in Tacitus' much-vaunted terseness.

September 29—I went to school for the first time to-day. I confess I was disappointed. We are reading, in the Fourth Division, in which I was placed at my mother's express request, Eutropius and Ovid; both very insipid writers. The boys are lamentably backward and show a deplorable lack of interest in the classics. The French master has an accent that leaves much to be desired, and he seems rather shaky about his past participles. However, all these things are but trifles. What I really resent is the gross injustice which seems to be the leading principle at this school—if school it can be called.

For instance, when the master asks a question, those boys who know the answer are told to hold up their hands. During the history lesson Henry VIII. was mentioned in connection with the religious quarrels of the sixteenth century, a question which, I confess, can but have small interest for any educated person at the present day. The master asked what British poet had written a play on the subject of Henry VIII. I, of course, held up my hand, and so did a boy called Jonas Pike. I was told to answer first, and I said that the play was in the main by Fletcher, with possible later interpolations. The usher, it is scarcely credible, said, "Go to the bottom of the form," and when Jonas Pike was asked he replied, "Shakespeare," and was told to go up one. This was, I consider, a monstrous piece of injustice.

During one of the intervals, which are only too frequent, between the lessons, the boys play a foolish game called "It," in which even those who have no aptitude and still less inclination for this tedious form of horse-play, are compelled to take part. The game consists in one boy being named "it" (though why the neuter is used in this case instead of the obviously necessary masculine it is hard to see). He has to endeavour to touch one of the other boys, who in their turn do their best to evade him by running, and should he succeed in touching one of them, the boy who is touched becomes "it" ipso facto. It is all very tedious and silly. I was touched almost immediately, and when I said that I would willingly transfer the privilege of being touched to one of the other boys who were obviously eager to obtain it, one of the bigger boys (again Jonas Pike) gave me a sharp kick on the shin. I confess I was ruffled. I was perhaps to blame in what followed. I am, perhaps, inclined to forget at times that Providence has made me physically strong. I retaliated with more insistence than I intended, and in the undignified scuffle which ensued Jonas Pike twisted his ankle. He had to be supported home. When questioned as to the cause of the accident I regret to say he told a deliberate falsehood. He said he had slipped on the ladder in the gymnasium. I felt it my duty to inform the head-master of the indirect and unwilling part I had played in the matter.

The head master, who is positively unable to perceive the importance of plain-speaking, said, "I suppose you mean you did it." I answered, "No, sir; I was the resisting but not the passive agent in an unwarrantable assault." The result was I was told to stay in during the afternoon and copy out the First Eclogue of Virgil. It is characteristic of the head master to choose a feeble Eclogue of Virgil instead of one of the admirable Georgics. Jonas Pike is to be flogged, as soon as his foot is well, for his untruthfulness.

This, my first experience of school life, is not very hopeful.

October 10—The routine of the life here seems to me more and more meaningless. The work is to me child's play; and indeed chiefly consists in checking the inaccuracies of the ushers. They show no gratitude to me—indeed, sometimes the reverse of gratitude.

One day, in the English class, one of the ushers grossly misquoted Pope. He said, "A little knowledge is a dangerous thing." I held up my hand and asked if the line was not rather "A little learning is a dangerous thing," adding that Pope would scarcely have thought a little knowledge to be dangerous, since all knowledge is valuable. The usher tried to evade the point by a joke, which betrayed gross theological ignorance. He said: "All Popes are not infallible."

One of the boys brought into school a foolish toy—a gutta-percha snake that contracts under pressure and expands when released, with a whistling screech.

Jonas Pike, who is the most ignorant as well as the most ill-mannered of all the boys, suggested that the snake should be put into the French master's locker, in which he keeps the exercises for the week. The key of the locker is left in charge of the top boy of the class, who, I say it in all modesty, is myself. Presently another boy, Hudson by name, asked me for the key. I gave it to him, and he handed it to Pike, who inserted the snake in the locker. When the French master opened the locker the snake flew in his face. He asked me if I had had any hand in the matter. I answered that I had not touched the snake. He asked me if I had opened the locker; I, of course, said "No." Questioned further as to how the snake could have got there, I admitted having lent the key to Hudson, ignorant of any ulterior purpose. In spite of this I was obliged, in company with Pike and Hudson, to copy out some entirely old-fashioned and meaningless exercises in syntax.

October 13—A pretty little episode happened at home to-day. The gardener's boy asked me if he might try his new axe on the old cherry-tree, which I have often vainly urged mother to cut down. I said, "By all means." It appears that he misunderstood me and cut down the tree. My mother was about to send him away, but I went straight to her and said I would take the entire responsibility for the loss of the tree on myself, as I had always openly advocated its removal and that the gardener's boy was well aware of my views on the subject. My mother was so much touched at my straightforwardness that she gave me some candy, a refreshment to which I am still partial. Would that the ushers at school could share her fine discrimination, her sound judgment, and her appreciation of character.

CHAPTER VI

FROM THE DIARY OF MARCUS AURELIUS

Rome. The Ides of March—It is curious that Julius Cæsar should have considered this date to be unlucky! It was on that—for him auspicious—date that he was for ever prevented from committing the egregious folly of accepting the crown of Rome. A king of Rome is an unthinkable thing! An emperor of the Roman Empire is, of course, a very different matter.

April 1—Faustina, in accordance with some ridiculous tradition, committed a grossly undignified act. She came into my study, the third hour—my busiest time, and asked me to lend her the memoirs of Remus in the Wolf's Lair. I spent a fruitless half-hour in search of the book. It then occurred to me that the whole matter was a jest—in the very worst taste, since both my secretaries were present—and I regret to say they smiled.

April 6—Went to the games, in company with Faustina and Commodus. Commodus, as usual, too exuberant in the manner of his applause. I am all in favour of his applauding. The games are not what they used to be. The modern lions consume the Christians without the slightest discrimination. All this modern hurry and hustle is very distressing.

April 10—Stayed at Tivoli with V.... and A.... from Saturday to Monday. Even in a country house a day may be well spent. Much interesting talk on the Fiscal question. V.... deprecates Tariff Reform in all its shapes. A.... while remaining, as he ever was, a staunch Free Trader, considers that in some cases—and given certain conditions —retaliation is admissible—possibly in the matter of the fringes of litters and the axles of chariot-wheels—-objects which exclusively concern the very rich.

April 20—An exhilarating day. Walked to the Tiber and back. Read the preface of the new Persian grammar. Faustina interrupted me three times over purely trivial matters of domestic detail.

April 20—Commodus is impossible. He grows more and more extravagant every day. He persists in spending his pocket money in buying absurd pets—and the gods know that Faustina has enough pets in the house already. But I am thankful to say I have drawn the line at badgers. I put my foot down. I was dignified, but firm. I endure Faustina's peacocks, because I think it is good for my better nature. Besides which they are ornamental and—if properly dressed—not unpleasant to the palate, but badgers—!

April 20—A painful episode occurred. When I returned from my morning stroll I was aware that an altercation was taking place in the atrium. I entered and found myself face to face with two Persian merchants—of the lowest type—who were exhibiting to Faustina several ropes of pearls. Faustina, of course, had had no hand in the matter. The merchants had forced themselves on her presence on some ridiculous pretext. Faustina, in spite of her faults, values jewels at their true price. She has a soul above such things. She abhors trinkets. She sees their futility.

April 23—Re-read the Iliad. Find it too long. The character of Helen shows defective psychology. Homer did not understand women.

April 27—Games again. Very tame. Lions lethargic as usual. How dissatisfied Nero would have been! Nero, although a bad poet, was an excellent organiser. He understood the psychology of the crowd. He was essentially an altruist. Faustina insisted on making a foolish bet. Women's bets are the last word of silliness. They bet because the name of a gladiator reminds them of a pet dog, or for some such reason. They have no inkling of logic: no power of deduction. I found no difficulty in anticipating the victories of the successful candidates, but I refrained from making a wager.

May 1—Absurd processions in the streets. Faustina painted her face black and walked round the garden in a movable bower of greenery. I could see no kind of point or sense in the episode. Under cross-examination, she confessed that the idea had been suggested to her by her nurse. All this is very trying. It sets Commodus the worst possible example. But I suppose I must endure this. The ways of Fate are inscrutable, and after all, things might have been worse. Faustina might have been a loose woman! A profligate!

May 6—Read out the first canto of my epic on the origins of species to Faustina and Commodus. Commodus, I regret to say, yawned and finally dozed. Faustina enjoyed it immensely. She said she always thought that I was a real poet, and that now she knew it. She says she thinks it is far better than Homer or Virgil; that there is so much more in it. Faustina is a very good judge of literature. There is no one whose opinion on matters of art and literature I value more. For instance she thinks Sappho's lyrics are not only trivial, but coarse. She also thinks Æschylus much overrated, which, of course, he is. How far we have got beyond all that! Some day I mean to write a play on the subject of love. It has never yet been properly treated—on the stage. Sophocles and Seneca knew nothing of women; and Euripides' women are far too complicated.

May 12—Meditated on religion, but was again interrupted by Faustina just as I was making a really illuminating note on the subject of Isis. Much distressed by modern free thought. Commodus pays much too much attention to the minor goddesses, but this, at his age, is excusable. He is, thank goodness, entirely untainted by the detestable Jewish or so-called "Christian" superstition, which I fear is spreading.

May 13—V.... and A.... dined. Also a Greek philosopher whose name escapes me. The Greek was most indiscreet. He discussed the Christian question before everybody. He must have been aware by my expression that the topic is one which I consider unfit for public discussion. He not only discussed, but he actually defended this hysterical, obstinate, unpatriotic, and fundamentally criminal sect. I do not, of course, entirely credit the stories current with regard to their orgies and their human sacrifices. The evidence is not—so far—sufficiently sound; but, whatever their practices and their rites may be, the Christians are a pernicious and dangerous sect. They will prove, unless they are extirpated, the ruin of the Empire. They have no notion of civic duty; no reverence, no respect for custom or tradition. They are unfilial, and they are the enemies of the human race. They are a cancer in the State. Faustina agrees with me, I am glad to say.

May 14—Commodus is suspected of having made friends with a Christian slave. The rumour is no doubt a calumny. I cannot bring myself to believe that a son of mine, with the education which he has enjoyed, and the example which has ever been before his eyes, of his father's unswerving and unremitting devotion to duty and the State, can have degraded himself by dabbling in this degrading and wicked superstition. Nevertheless it is as well to be on the safe side, and, after prolonged reflection, I have decided to make a great sacrifice. I am going to allow him to take part professionally in the games: under another name of course. I think it may distract him. The games are a Roman institution. They are the expression of the Empire. They breathe the spirit of Romulus, of Brutus, of Regulus, of Fabius Cunctator, of Cincinnatus, of the Gracchi. Faustina said only yesterday that she felt she was the mother of at least one Gracchus! That was well said. I was much touched.

May 20—Commodus has appeared with great success, but the Lions still show apathy.

CHAPTER VII

FROM THE DIARY OF MRS JAMES LEE'S HUSBAND

October 1—At last the heat wave is over. It's the first day we have been able to breathe for months.

Just as I was coming back from my morning walk, Hilda leant out of the window, and suggested I could climb up into her room like Romeo. I said I preferred the door. Hilda shut the window with a bang and was cross all through luncheon.

"Rissoles again," I said to Hilda, "you know I hate hashed meat." She said: "I know I can't give you the food you get at the Grand Hotel." That's because I went to Deauville last week.

October 5—We lit a fire for the first time last night. Hilda said she felt cold. I thought it was rather stuffy. She said: "Do light the fire," and went out of the room. I lit it, and it smoked. This chimney always does smoke at first. When she came back she said: "What have you done?" I said: "I've lit the fire; you asked me to." She said: "But not all that wood at once, and you ought to have pushed the wood back." For the rest of the evening she complained of the heat and the smoke, although we had the window open in the dining room and the smoke had all disappeared after a few moments.

October 7—It's very windy. Went for a walk on the cliffs. Back through the fields. Saw a rabbit and a magpie. Wish I had had a gun.

I said to Hilda that the sea was striped to leeward like a snake, and olive-coloured, but on the weather side it was spotted with wind. Hilda said: "You are very observant about the weather." This was a hit at me and the fire. Little things rankle in her mind.

Afterwards she was sorry she had said this and she said: "What fun we shall have here in winter." I don't think it's a winter place myself, but I want to stay here till I've finished my poem. I'm getting on with it.

October 8—I read out to Hilda a lyric I had just finished. It's to come in the Second Canto when Lancelot says good-bye to Princess Asra. The situation is roughly that the Princess bullies him and he gets sick of it and goes—and then, of course, she's sorry, when it's too late. He sings the song as he's going. She overhears it. I was rather pleased with it. Hilda said: "Oh! of course I know I worry you with my attentions." What this had got to do with the poem I can't think. It was all because last night, when I was working, Hilda came into my room and said: "Are you warm enough?" and I said "Yes," rather absent-mindedly, as I was in the middle of my work. Ten minutes later she looked in again and asked me if I wanted some beer, and I said "No," without looking up. Then very soon afterwards she came in a third time, and asked me if I was sure I wasn't cold, and whether I wouldn't have the fire lit. Rather snappishly—because it is a bore to be interrupted just when one's on the verge of getting an idea fixed—I said "No."

I'm afraid this hurt her feelings.

October 9—Since Hilda has given up her sketching she has nothing to do. I was very busy this afternoon finishing my weekly article in time for the post. She rushed into the room and said didn't I think a butterfly settling on a jock was the ultimate symbol of love and the mind of man? I said I thought she was very probably right. Heavens knows what she meant. Women's minds move by jerks, one never knows what they'll say next. They're so irrelevant.

October 10—It's blowing a gale. Stuck in the poem. Hilda says it's cynical. I don't know what she means. She says she didn't know I was so bitter. I said: "It's only a kind of fairy tale." She said: "Yes; but that makes it worse." "But it's only an ordinary love story," I said. She said: "Of course I know nothing can go on being the same. It can no doubt be better, but not the same as it was before." "But Princess Asra is only an incident in my poem," I said. Hilda said nothing, but after a time she asked me whether I thought that was the meaning of the moan of the wind. I have no idea what she meant by "that." She is very cryptic sometimes.

October 11—Lovely day. The sun came out and I suggested that I should take a holiday, and that we should go and have a picnic on the rocks. I was afraid Hilda might have something against the plan—one never knows. But she didn't. On the contrary she seemed delighted. She made a hamper and I carried it down to the rocks. We caught shrimps and threw stones into the sea just like children. I think Hilda enjoyed herself. On the way home, I asked her why she didn't go on with her drawing. I really think it's a great pity she has given it up. She has real talent. She said: "I will if you wish it." I said: "Of course I don't want you to do it, if you don't like; but I do think it's a pity to waste such a very real talent." She said: "I quite understand," and sighed. I wonder what she was thinking of. Hilda is absurdly modest. She draws extremely well, especially figures.

October 12—Hilda has begun drawing again. I am delighted. She began copying the cast of a hand; but I suggested to her that it would be far more interesting for her to draw a real hand from nature. So she got a little girl from the village to sit for her. I am delighted. It gives her an occupation, and I really am very busy just now. After all, we came here so as not to be disturbed—to be away from people and interruptions; and I find that in the last two months I have got through less work than I did in London in June. I must make up for lost time. I can't get on with the poem. I think I shall leave it for a time. I should immensely like Hilda's opinion on what ought to happen next. She can be of the greatest help and use when she chooses. Unfortunately she has taken one of those unreasonable and entirely unaccountable dislikes to this poem, and no argument is of the slightest use. It's no good even mentioning it. I shall leave it for a time and go on with my other work. It is most unfortunate that Hilda should look upon it in this light, especially as she doesn't even know what the subject is; but she has taken an episode—in fact, one little song—as symbolic of the whole. But then logic never was Hilda's strong point.

October 13—Hilda is getting on very well with the hand. She seems to enjoy it, which is the great thing.

October 24—Have been too busy all these last days thinking, even to write my diary. Believe I have at last really got an idea for the poem. Shall begin to-morrow. Have not dared mention it to Hilda. Fortunately she is still utterly absorbed in her drawing.

October 27—Great disappointment. Last night Hilda said it was no good concealing things any longer, and that one must look facts in the face. I had no idea what she meant. Then she said she had noticed for some time past how bored I was here, and how I was longing to get rid of her. Nothing I could say would persuade her of the contrary. I tried to explain that I had been searching for a new idea and that this had no doubt made me appear more absent-minded than usual. She said: "I am not going to worry you any longer. I am going to set you free." And to my intense surprise she announced that she had booked a berth on the steamer for the day after to-morrow. I knew that argument wouldn't be of any use, so I gave in at once. It is most disappointing just as I had got an idea I wanted to consult her about.

October 29—On board the steamer Queen Marguerite. Saw Hilda off. She insisted on going and refused to argue. Deeply regret she is leaving. Hilda is the only woman I ever met who remains tidy even on a steamer. The sea-air suits her. It has done her a world of good, and it's a great pity she is leaving so soon—she says it's for good; but that, of course, is ridiculous.

CHAPTER VIII

FROM THE DIARY OF SHERLOCK HOLMES

Baker Street, January 1—Starting a diary in order to jot down a few useful incidents which will be of no use to Watson. Watson very often fails to see that an unsuccessful case is more interesting from a professional point of view than a successful case. He means well.

January 6—Watson has gone to Brighton for a few days, for change of air. This morning quite an interesting little incident happened which I note as a useful example of how sometimes people who have no powers of deduction nevertheless stumble on the truth for the wrong reason. (This never happens to Watson, fortunately.) Lestrade called from Scotland Yard with reference to the theft of a diamond and ruby ring from Lady Dorothy Smith's wedding presents. The facts of the case were briefly these: On Thursday evening such of the presents as were jewels had been brought down from Lady Dorothy's bedroom to the drawing-room to be shown to an admiring group of friends. The ring was amongst them. After they had been shown, the jewels were taken upstairs once more and locked in the safe. The next morning the ring was missing. Lestrade, after investigating the matter, came to the conclusion that the ring had not been stolen, but had either been dropped in the drawing-room, or replaced in one of the other cases; but since he had searched the room and the remaining cases, his theory so far received no support. I accompanied him to Eaton Square to the residence of Lady Middlesex, Lady Dorothy's mother.

While we were engaged in searching the drawing-room, Lestrade uttered a cry of triumph and produced the ring from the lining of the arm-chair. I told him he might enjoy the triumph, but that the matter was not quite so simple as he seemed to think. A glance at the ring had shown me not only that the stones were false, but that the false ring had been made in a hurry. To deduce the name of its maker was of course child's play. Lestrade or any pupil of Scotland Yard would have taken for granted it was the same jeweller who had made the real ring. I asked for the bridegroom's present, and in a short time I was interviewing the jeweller who had provided it. As I thought, he had made a ring, with imitation stones (made of the dust of real stones), a week ago, for a young lady. She had given no name and had fetched and paid for it herself. I deduced the obvious fact that Lady Dorothy had lost the real ring, her uncle's gift, and, not daring to say so, had had an imitation ring made. I returned to the house, where I found Lestrade, who had called to make arrangements for watching the presents during their exhibition.

I asked for Lady Dorothy, who at once said to me:

"The ring was found yesterday by Mr Lestrade."

"I know," I answered, "but which ring?"

She could not repress a slight twitch of the eyelids as she said: "There was only one ring."

I told her of my discovery and of my investigations.

"This is a very odd coincidence, Mr Holmes," she said. "Some one else must have ordered an imitation. But you shall examine my ring for yourself." Where-upon she fetched the ring, and I saw it was no imitation. She had of course in the meantime found the real ring.

But to my intense annoyance she took it to Lestrade and said to him:

"Isn't this the ring you found yesterday, Mr Lestrade?"

Lestrade examined it and said, "Of course it is absolutely identical in every respect."

"And do you think it is an imitation?" asked this most provoking young lady.

"Certainly not," said Lestrade, and turning to me he added: "Ah! Holmes, that is where theory leads one. At the Yard we go in for facts."

I could say nothing; but as I said good-bye to Lady Dorothy, I congratulated her on having found the real ring. The incident, although it proved the correctness of my reasoning, was vexing as it gave that ignorant blunderer an opportunity of crowing over me.

January 10—A man called just as Watson and I were having breakfast. He didn't give his name. He asked me if I knew who he was. I said, "Beyond seeing that you are unmarried, that you have travelled up this morning from Sussex, that you have served in the French Army, that you write for reviews, and are especially interested in the battles of the Middle Ages, that you give lectures, that you are a Roman Catholic, and that you have once been to Japan, I don't know who you are."

The man replied that he was unmarried, but that he lived in Manchester, that he had never been to Sussex or Japan, that he had never written a line in his life, that he had never served in any army save the English Territorial force, that so far from being a Roman Catholic he was a Freemason, and that he was by trade an electrical engineer—I suspected him of lying; and I asked him why his boots were covered with the clayey and chalk mixture peculiar to Horsham; why his boots were French Army service boots, elastic-sided, and bought probably at Valmy; why the second half of a return ticket from Southwater was emerging from his ticket-pocket; why he wore the medal of St Anthony on his watch-chain; why he smoked Caporal cigarettes; why the proofs of an article on the Battle of Eylau were protruding from his breast-pocket, together with a copy of the Tablet; why he carried in his hand a parcel which, owing to the untidy way in which it had been made (an untidiness which, in harmony with the rest of his clothes, showed that he could not be married) revealed the fact that it contained photographic magic lantern slides; and why he was tattooed on the left wrist with a Japanese fish.

"The reason I have come to consult you will explain some of these things," he answered.

"I was staying last night at the Windsor Hotel, and this morning when I woke up I found an entirely different set of clothes from my own. I called the waiter and pointed this out, but neither the waiter nor any of the other servants, after making full enquiries, were able to account for the change. None of the other occupants of the hotel had complained of anything being wrong with their own clothes.

"Two gentlemen had gone out early from the hotel at 7.30. One of them had left for good, the other was expected to return.

"All the belongings I am wearing, including this parcel, which contains slides, belong to someone else.

"My own things contained nothing valuable, and consisted of clothes and boots very similar to these; my coat was also stuffed with papers. As to the tattoo, it was done at a Turkish bath by a shampooer, who learnt the trick in the Navy."

The case did not present any features of the slightest interest. I merely advised the man to return to the hotel and await the real owner of the clothes, who was evidently the man who had gone out at 7.30.

This is a case of my reasoning being, with one partial exception, perfectly correct. Everything I had deduced would no doubt have fitted the real owner of the clothes.

Watson asked rather irrelevantly why I had not noticed that the clothes were not the man's own clothes.

A stupid question, as the clothes were reach-me-downs which fitted him as well as such clothes ever do fit, and he was probably of the same build as their rightful owner.

January 12—Found a carbuncle of unusual size in the plum-pudding. Suspected the makings of an interesting case. But luckily, before I had stated any hypothesis to Watson—who was greatly excited— Mrs Turner came in and noticed it and said her naughty nephew Bill had been at his tricks again, and that the red stone had come from a Christmas tree. Of course, I had not examined the stone with my lens.

CHAPTER IX

FROM THE DIARY OF THE EMPEROR TITUS

Titus reginam Berenicem ... cui etiam nuptias pollicitus ferebatur ... statim ab urbe demisit invitus invitam. —TACITUS.

Rome, Monday—The eruption at Vesuvius does not after all appear to have been greatly exaggerated, as I at first had thought on receiving Pliny's graphic letter. One never can quite trust literary men when facts are in question. It is clear that I missed a very fine and interesting spectacle. In fact I have lost a day. Good phrase, that. Must try and bring it in some time or other.

Tuesday—I fear there is no doubt of Berenice's growing unpopularity. It is tiresome, as I was hoping that the marriage might take place soon—quietly. She insists on wearing a diadem—which is unnecessary; and her earrings—made of emeralds and gold cupids—are too large. She asked me, to-day, if I didn't think she resembled the Rose of Sharon. I said I supposed she meant the rose of Paestum. She said, "Ah! You've never read the Song of Songs." I said I had read all Sappho. She said, "It's not by Sappho, it's by Solomon." I had no idea King Solomon wrote.

Wednesday—Berenice has asked some of her relations to stay with her. They arrived this morning. Her mother, her sister, her younger brother, and her cousin. They are very conversational. They chatter together like parrots or cockatoos. They are also insatiably inquisitive. Talked finance with Paulinus. He says that the Treasury is practically empty. Nobody in the palace appears to have any ready money. When the usual crowd of beggars came to the palace this evening for their daily allowance I had to send them away. It was the first time, Paulinus remarked, that I had let a day go by without making a gift. "Yes," I answered, "I have lost a day." The phrase, I am glad to say, was heard by everybody. I afterwards borrowed a little money from Berenice's brother, who made no difficulties. He is a nice, generous lad, if a little talkative, but then we all of us have our faults. Berenice's mother loses no opportunity of asking when the wedding day is to be. Most awkward. I temporised.

Thursday—Berenice's relations have spread the news in the Court, by telling it to one of the matrons in strict confidence, that I am about to marry Berenice almost immediately. This is most unfortunate. The news has created a sensation, and they all say that such a match would be more than unpopular amongst the people. Berenice has not mentioned it herself. Lost heavily at dice yesterday. Accepted the offer of Berenice's brother to lend me a lump sum, instead of constantly borrowing small coins. I have no doubt that is the wiser course.

Thursday, a week later—The strain on my purse is terrible. Had, of course, to subscribe largely to the Pompeii and Herculaneum fund, also to the pestilence relief, also to the Flavian Amphitheatre fund. Borrowed another lump sum from Berenice's brother. He is certainly very good-natured. Berenice's mother again referred to the marriage question. I said this was an unlucky month for marriages. "Not if you are born in December," she answered. Unfortunately I was born in December.

Friday—Do not know where to turn for money. Do not always want to be borrowing from Berenice's brother. Somehow or other it makes them all so familiar. Given the circumstances, and the extreme unpopularity of their presence here, it is awkward. Besides, it is a shame to trade on the good-nature of a youth. Have sold all the decorations of the Imperial residence and devoted a portion of the proceeds to the Relief Fund. Some one spread the rumour among the dear people that I had devoted the whole of the money to the Relief Fund. I cannot think how these rumours get about.

Saturday, a week later—This has been a most expensive fortnight. Have had to do a lot of entertaining, and I regret to say I have been once more obliged to borrow a lump sum from Berenice's brother. How I shall ever be able to pay him back the gods alone know! Had the news of my marriage unofficially announced, followed immediately by a semi-official and ambiguous denial, made to see what effect the news would have among the public. Paulinus says the impression produced was deplorable. The Romans cannot, he says, forget that Berenice is a queen. Of course they can't, if she will wear a crown. People say, he says, that even Nero and Caligula avoided offending public opinion on this point. They refer also to Julius Cæsar's action on the Lupercal. There is no doubt that such a course will ensure me a lasting unpopularity. But what is to be done? Berenice's relations talk of the marriage as a matter of course. I have practically promised marriage. Berenice herself says nothing, but her silence is eloquent. Her brother becomes more and more familiar, and presses me to accept further loans. I do my best to refuse, and I have made a vow that the lump sum which he lent me to-day shall be positively the last one.

Monday—Paulinus tells me that the Senate have decided to present me with a monster petition against my marriage. Since it is obviously impossible—owing to the strong feeling raised and the present excited state of popular opinion—I have resolved to anticipate events, and I have given leave to Paulinus to contradict officially the rumours of my impending marriage. He is to add (unofficially) that Berenice is shortly leaving Rome for change of air; and that she will probably spend the summer months in her charming villa on the Dead Sea. In the meantime I have got to break the news to Berenice before to-morrow morning. Antiochus, the king of Commagene, arrived here this morning. More expense!

Monday night, later—The crisis is partially over. It has been extremely painful. Berenice at first was incredulous. Then she was upset, and left me, threatening to kill herself. I sent Paulinus to try and calm her. She then said she would leave Rome without setting eyes on me again, and state her reasons in an open letter which she would issue for private circulation only. This, of course, would have been most undesirable. Her mother and sister backed her up, and threw up at me the example of Antony, taunting me with cowardice, of being afraid of the Senate, and of outraging the dignity of a family, royal in rank, and of immemorial lineage. (Berenice is directly descended from King Solomon on her mother's side.) Finally, Berenice's brother came to me and said that as he would shortly be leaving Rome he would be obliged if I could pay him back the trifling loans he had favoured me with. He brought a list of them. He charges interest. It is a tradition, he says, in his family, to charge 90 per cent, interest on Royal loans. He said that he was quite willing to apply to the Senate, if the reimbursement in any way incommoded me. This was a great shock to me. Immediate repayment was and is impossible. The marriage is equally impossible. I told Berenice frankly that I could not remain in Rome as Emperor and the husband of a foreign Queen. She said, "But why shouldn't I be Empress?" Woman-like, she missed the point. I said I was willing to follow her to her villa and renounce all claim to the Empire. Having offered her this alternative, I summoned Antiochus, who is an old friend of hers, to be the arbiter. As soon as the facts were put before him I left them and Antiochus had a lengthy interview with Berenice in private. I was convinced this was the best course. At the end of it, Berenice generously refused to accept my sacrifice, and while renouncing all idea of self-slaughter or retaliation announced her intention of leaving Rome. But those loans! and their terrible interest! that matter is still unsettled!

Tuesday—All has been settled. Antiochus has lent me the whole sum due to Berenice's brother, and a handsome margin for my personal use. I restored the interest and capital of the loan to Berenice's brother. Said farewell to the family before the whole Court, and handed Berenice's brother a fine gold chain as a slight token of my esteem. "This," he said, "is too much." "No man," I answered, "should leave his prince's presence dissatisfied." Hereupon the whole Court murmured applause, and by a slight gesture I indicated that the audience was at an end. Berenice, alas! left Rome at noon, escorted by Antiochus, who is to spend the summer with her in Palestine. To-day I can say in all conscientiousness that I have not lost a day; but it seems to me that I have lost everything else that there is to lose in this life.

CHAPTER X

FROM THE DIARY OF HARRIET SHELLEY

George Street, Edinburgh, September 6, 1811—Mr Hogg arrived this morning. He seemed at first to be quite oblivious of the fact that he was in the city of the unfortunate Queen Mary. Bysshe and I conducted him to the palace of Holyrood immediately, where we inspected the instructive and elegant series of portraits of the Scottish kings. I was much affected by the sight of the unfortunate Queen's bedroom.

Mr Hogg has not been well grounded in history; and he was on more than one occasion inaccurate. He had never heard of Fergus the Just. Bysshe was much moved, and enchanted by the objects of interest. He ran through the rooms at a great pace, now and then pointing back at an object of interest and exclaiming: "That is good." I regretted the absence of Eliza, but perhaps it is as well that she was not with us on this occasion. She would not have permitted me to contemplate the tragic stain of Rizzio's wound, for fear of the effect the sight might have on my nerves. Mr Hogg was strangely insensible to the sorrowful associations of the spot.

After we had inspected the rooms and the relics, Bysshe with intent, I, with renewed awe, and Mr Hogg with a somewhat inopportune levity, Bysshe was obliged to go home and write letters, and so I suggested that Mr Hogg should conduct me to Arthur's Seat, in order to enjoy the sublime prospect which that eminence commands.

So sublime, so grand, so inspiring was the view that even Mr Hogg was impressed. As for myself, words fail to express the manifold and conflicting emotions which were stirred in my breast. The weather was fine, clear and tranquil; but alas! no sooner had we started on our descent than the wind began to blow with great violence. It was of course impossible for me in such circumstances to risk the impropriety which might be occasioned, had the wind, as was only too probable, so disturbed my dress as to reveal to my companion the indelicate spectacle of my decently concealed ankles, so I seated myself on a rock resolving to wait until the violence of the wind should subside. Mr Hogg, who laid unnecessary stress on the fact that he had not dined on either of the preceding days, and being deficient in a proper sense of delicacy and seemliness, vowed he would desert me and proceed home by himself. To my dismay he began to carry his threat into execution, and it was with the utmost difficulty that I succeeded in accomplishing the descent without affording him any unseemly exhibition.

Sunday—The manner in which the Sabbath is observed in this city is repellent to my principles. Bysshe and Mr Hogg have gone to the Kirk. I pleaded the wearisome performance would be certain in my case to bring on a headache and so I remained at home. They returned much exhausted by the wrestlings of an eminent divine with Satan. I am engaged in translating Madame Cottin's immortal "Claire D'Albe" into English prose. This occupies my morning. Bysshe is translating a treatise of Buffon, with which we were both of us charmed. In the evenings I read out "Telemachus."

I regret to say that Bysshe fell asleep while I was but half way through an instructive discourse of Idomeneius relating to the wise laws of Crete. Mr Hogg is an attentive listener and it is a pleasure to read to him.

York, October 10, 1811—Travelled by post-chaise from Darlington. Read "Anna St Ives" by Holcroft in the chaise throughout the journey. Bysshe was restless and suggested my skipping certain portions of the narrative. I, of course, declined, knowing that it was the intention of the authoress that her work should be read without omissions. Bysshe is obliged to go to London. In the evenings I read out Dr Robertson's historical works to Mr Hogg. We are on the eve of a great event. My dear sister Eliza has consented to visit us and is about to arrive. What a privilege for Mr Hogg, what a source of pleasure for Bysshe. I ardently regret that he should not be present to welcome her.

October 25—Eliza has arrived. I am deeply touched by her kindness in coming and overcome when I think what a joyful surprise her presence will be for Bysshe, and how it will illuminate our household.

October 26—Bysshe arrived from London. Eliza spent the day brushing her hair. In the evening I suggested reading aloud from Holcroft; but Eliza, such is her kind-heartedness, feared that it might upset my nerves. She felt certain too, that her esteemed friend, Miss Warne, whom she regards as a pattern and model in all things, would not approve of Holcroft.

October 26—Eliza is certain that Miss Warne would find nothing to admire in York Minster. Changed our lodgings. Eliza thinks that the pure mountain air of the Lakes would be salutary to my nerves. Bysshe and Mr Hogg miss our evening readings. I sometimes, however, continue to read to them in an undertone when Eliza is brushing her hair. But the pleasure is marred by the trepidation I am in lest I should disturb her. Eliza objects to the name Bysshe. She is certain Miss Warne could not endure such a name, so in future my husband shall be called Percy. It is certainly prettier and more romantic.

Keswick, November 16—We have made the acquaintance of the Southeys. Mr Southey is a great reader and devotes two hours daily to the study of the Portuguese and Spanish languages. Mrs Southey is an adept at book-binding and binds her husband's books with elegance and neatness. Bysshe, I mean Percy, has alas three times narrowly risked offending the poet. The first time by inadvertently taking a book down from one of his book-shelves, the second time by falling asleep when Mr Southey after having locked him into his study was reading aloud to him his epic, "The Curse of Kehama," and the third time by sharply criticising his action in eating tea-cakes, and by subsequently devouring a whole plate of them, himself.

Bysshe, I mean Percy, has implored me to beg Mrs Southey to instruct me in the art of making tea-cakes. I wish Eliza could begin to realise the existence of Bysshe, I mean Percy. She seems altogether unaware of his presence in the house; but then Eliza is so much occupied in considering what will be best for me that she has no time to bestow any attention to anything else. Percy is contemplating the composition of a poem which is to be called "Queen Mab." Eliza said that Miss Warne had a horror of "Queen Mab"; Bysshe explained to her that his poem was to be didactic and philosophical and had nothing to do with fairies. "That," said Eliza, "makes it worse." Bysshe ran out of the room with shrill exclamation of impatience. "Hush, hush!" said Eliza, "think of poor Harriet's nerves."

November 20—Bysshe confessed to me that he could see neither beauty nor charm in Eliza. This is curious since her black hair has always been an object of universal admiration. I am afraid that Eliza does not understand him. I need hardly say what a disappointment this is to me.

Bysshe and I were thinking of writing a novel in collaboration. But Eliza said that Miss Warne considered that it was not seemly for a woman to dabble in fiction. Bysshe, I mean Percy—(In writing I find it difficult to accustom myself to the new name, but I am fortunately successful in the presence of Eliza in always saying Percy)—Percy and I are thinking of studying Hebrew. I have not yet told Eliza of this project. She is opposed to my reading Latin authors in their original tongue.

November 30—We were walking this afternoon in the neighbourhood of the lake. Percy, Eliza and myself. Percy was talking of Plato's republic when Eliza interrupted him by recalling to his mind something which she had indeed often mentioned before, namely, Miss Warne's positive dislike of all the Greek authors and especially Plato. Scarcely had she uttered these words, when we looked round and found that Bysshe had vanished in silence like a ghost in the trees. We called and searched for him in vain.

But when we returned to the house we found him awaiting us buried in a book.

The incident greatly displeased Eliza and she insisted upon my taking to my bed as soon as we got home, although I confess I felt no suspicion of any ailment, nor would she hear of my reading either aloud or to myself. She sat by my bed-side, brushing her hair. She grieved me by saying that she could not conceive what Miss Warne would think of Bysshe. I mean Percy.

CHAPTER XI

FROM THE "JOURNAL INTIME" OF THE EMPEROR TIBERIUS

February 1—Disquieting news from Parthia. Artabanus is giving trouble again. Shall probably have to send an expedition. The military party in Rome say that there will probably be unrest in Thrace in the spring. I remember they said the same thing last year. Slept wretchedly last night. Claricles' medicine is worse than useless. Wrote three despatches and one private letter. Fed Hannibal, the tortoise. Went for a stroll in the afternoon. Picked the first wind-flower, and put it in water. The gardener says we shall have some rain shortly. Please the Gods this may be true, as the country needs it badly! Dined alone. Played spilikins after dinner with Fufius, but found it a strain.

February 2—Woke at four and remained awake until seven, then went asleep again, and overslept myself. Scolded Balbus for not calling me. He said he did not dare call me more emphatically. Told him it must not occur again.

February 3—Nothing particular.

February 4—Letter from my mother begging me to come and see her. Says she is suffering from lung trouble. Women are so unreasonable. She must realise that it is impossible for me to get away just at present. Hannibal would not touch his lettuce to-day. This is the third day running it has happened. Claricles has given him some medicine. Strolled along to cliffs in the morning. Much vexed by a fisherman who pushed a lobster under my very nose. I have a horror of shellfish. Varus and Aufidius dined. Found their conversation a strain. So retired early. Read the Seventh Book of the "Æneid," but found it insipid. Virgil will certainly not live. He was a sycophant.

February 10—Anniversary of poor Julia's death. Began to write short poem on the subject, but was interrupted by the arrival of the courier from Rome. Much vexed, as it altogether interrupted my train of thought and spoilt what would have been a fine elegy. News from Rome unsatisfactory. It rained in the afternoon, so I did not go out. Sorted my specimens of dried herbs, which are in a sad state of confusion. Dined alone. Dictated a despatch to Sejanus. Read some of the "Alcestis" (Euripides) before going to bed. Alcestis reminds me of Julia in many ways. She had the same fervid altruism and the same knack of saying really disagreeable things. But they both meant well....

March 1—A lovely spring day. Went for a stroll, and jotted down a few ideas for a poem on Spring. The birds were singing. Listened for some time to the babbling of the brook. Think of alluding to this in the poem. "Desilientis aquae" would make a good ending to a pentameter. Mentioned it to Fufius when I came in, casually. He said he did not think it was very original. Fufius is hyper-critical. He does not feel poetry. Finished the memorial lines on Julia ending "Ave atque Vale." Shall not show them to Fufius. He would be certain to say something disparaging. Positively haunted by the sight of the wild tulips in the hills, fluttering in the breeze. Sights like this live in the memory. Disturbed early in the morning by a noise of hammering. It is strange that where-ever I go this happens. Made inquiries, and ascertained that the stable roof is being repaired. If it is not the stable roof it is sure to be something else. Last week it was a strayed cow which woke me at five. Find it very difficult to get sleep in the early morning, whatever precautions I take. In a month's time the nightingales will begin, and then sleep will be out of the question. Thinking of writing a poem called "To Sleep."

March 10—Claricles says I am overworked and need a change. Have decided to go for a short walking tour, quite by myself. Thought of taking Fufius, but knowing how self-willed he is, decided not to. Packed my knapsack. Took an extra pair of sandals, a worsted scarf, an ivory comb, two gold toothpicks, and a volume of Sappho's Songs. Find this light, feminine verse suitable for outdoor life. Shall start early to-morrow. Had my hair cut. The slave was clumsy when cutting round the ears. They still smart. Find this fault to be universal among haircutters. Shall take tablets with me in order to jot down any ideas for future poems, although Claricles advises me to give up writing for two or three weeks.

March 13—Returned earlier than I expected. Walking tour successful on the whole. Visited Sorrentum, an idyllic spot. Not sure I don't prefer it to Capreæ. It is a curious thing that man is always discontented with what he has, and hankers after what he has not got. Walked leisurely the first day, stopping every now and then for light refreshment. Found the country people very civil and anxious to please. Nobody knew who I was, and I was intensely gratified by many spontaneous and frank experiences of loyalty and devotion to the Emperor. This is refreshing in this sceptical age. It is a comfort to think that although I may not go down to posterity as a great military genius like Julius Cæsar, I shall at least leave a blameless name, as far as my domestic life is concerned, and an untarnished reputation for benevolence, kindness, and unswerving devotion to duty. Without being conceited, I think that some of my verse will live. I think I shall be among the Roman poets when I die; but this is not saying much, when one considers the absurd praise given to poetasters such as Virgil and Ponticus. Strolling along the seashore near Sorrentum a very pretty little episode occurred. A woman, one of the fishermen's wives, was sitting by her cottage door, spinning. Her child, a little girl about six years old, was playing with a doll hard by.

I said "Good day" to the fisherman's wife, and she offered me a glass of wine. I declined, as Claricles has forbidden me red wine, but I said I would gladly accept a bowl of milk. She immediately went to fetch it, and the child went with her. When they returned the child offered me the bowl, lisping in a charming manner. I drank the milk, and the mother then said to the child:

"Tell the kind gentleman whom you love best in the world."

"Papa and mamma," lisped the child.

"And after that?" asked the mother.

"After that the divine Emperor Tiberius, who is the father and the mother of us all," she said.

I gave the mother a gold piece. Fufius says it is a mistake to give money to the poor, and that it pauperises them. He says one does more harm than good by indiscriminate charity. But I think it cannot be a bad thing to follow the impulses of the heart. I should like this to be said of me: "Although he had many faults, such as discontent and want of boldness, his heart was in the right place." It is little incidents like the one I noted above which make up for the many disappointments and trials of a monarch's life. The second day of my tour was marred by a thunder-shower, but I found a thrush's nest and three eggs in it. There are few things which move me so inexpressibly as the sight of a thrush's nest with the eggs lying in it. It is curious that the nightingale's egg should be so ugly. Owing to the bad weather, and the rheumatism in my joints which it brought on, I was obliged to cut short my tour.

(This extract probably belongs to a later period)

June—Asinius Gallus has again sent in a petition about the prison fare. It appears he has a conscientious objection to eating veal. The officials say they can do nothing. If they make an exception in his favour they will be obliged to do so in many less deserving cases. I confess these little things worry me. Our prison system seems to me lacking in elasticity; but it is dreadfully difficult to bring into effect any sweeping reform; because if the prison disciplinary system is modified to meet the requirements of the more cultivated prisoners, the prisons would be crowded with ruffians who would get themselves arrested on purpose. At least this is the official view, and it is shared by Sejanus, who has gone into the matter thoroughly. I confess it leaves me unconvinced. I am glad to say we are ahead of the Persians in the matter. In Persia they think nothing of shutting up a prisoner—of whatever rank—in a cell and keeping him isolated from the world sometimes for as long as three months at a time. This seems to me barbarous.

July 6—The heat is overpowering. Agrippina threatens to come home and to bring her daughter. I wrote saying I thought it is very unwise to bring children here at this time of year, owing to the prevalence of fever. She answered that her daughter was looking forward to the sea-bathing. If they come it will mean that my summer will be ruined.

July 7—I went to the home farm this afternoon. The farmer's wife is very ill. There is little or no hope of her recovery. Spent two hours there reading out passages of the "Odyssey." She does not understand Greek; but it seemed to soothe her. Her husband told her that he felt confident that she could not get worse after this. The faith of these simple folk is most touching. How unlike Fufius and all his friends.

August 1—There is no news except that, as always occurs at this time of year, the Phœnix is reported to have been seen in Egypt.

August 3—One of those distressing little incidents happened to-day which entirely spoil one's comfort and peace of mind for the moment: just like a piece of dust getting into one's eye. My old friend Lucius Anuseius came all the way from Rhodes to see me. By some mistake he was shown into the Chamber, where prisoners are examined, and before the error was rectified he was rather rudely interrogated. It turned out afterwards that Balbus mistook him for Titus Anuseius, the informer. Balbus is growing more and more stupid; he forgets everything. I ought to send him away; on the other hand, he knows my habits, and I should feel lost without him. As it is, Claricles says that Lucius is likely to feel it for several days. He is so sensitive and the slightest thing upsets his nerves. All his family are touchy, and I am afraid he will look upon the matter as a deliberate slight. If it had happened to anyone else it would not have mattered. They would have understood at once. This has quite put me out. But, as Fufius says, how little I shall think of this in a year's time.

August 7—Lucius Anuseius left the island in a huff. It is most regrettable.

August 12—Agrippina arrives to-morrow. There is nothing to be done. How pleasant life would be were it not for one's relations.

CHAPTER XII

FROM THE DIARY OF ŒDIPUS REX

Corinth. The Feast of the Minotaur—My birthday and coming-of-age. All went oft very successfully. Papa gave me a chariot and mamma a pocket tooth-pick, set in gold, with an Egyptian inscription on it (two flamingoes and a water-rat, which means in Egyptian "Be merry and wise"). Nausicaa, my nurse, gave me a stylus-wiper with "A Present from Corinth" beautifully worked into it in silk. Polyphemus, our faithful old messenger (who has only one eye), gave me a pair of sandal strings. Very useful, as I'm always losing mine.

In the morning, after I had received all the family congratulations and tokens, at the first meal, there was a public presentation of gifts in the palace.

The town of Corinth sent a deputation, headed by the Priest of the Temple of Castor and Pollux, which presented me, on behalf of the city, with a silver vase, symbolic of the freedom of the city, beautifully embossed, and engraved with a suitable inscription.

The priest made a long speech, and papa, who never cared for oratory, kept on muttering, "By Demeter, be brief," but the priest wasn't brief. He spoke for nearly an hour.

Then I had to respond. I said I would earnestly endeavour to follow in my father's footsteps and to deserve the good-will and esteem of my future subjects, which was being manifested in so touching and patriotic a fashion. My speech had all been written out for me beforehand by Zoroaster, my Persian tutor; but I flatter myself I added a few unexpected and telling touches.

For instance, I began by saying: "Unaccustomed as I am to speaking in public—." They cheered this to the echo.

I also managed to bring in rather an amusing anecdote about how a foreign merchant called Abraham tried to get the better of a Corinthian merchant in a bargain, and how the Corinthian got the best of him by guile. This provoked loud laughter.

My peroration, ending with the words:

"What do they know of Corinth who only Corinth know?"

(a quotation from Tyrtæus) was loudly cheered. But my cousin Thersites almost spoilt the effect by adding audibly, "Quite enough."

In the afternoon there were games, and an ox was roasted whole for the οἱ πολλὸι. Papa says, now I am of age, I must go and pay my respects to the oracle at Delphi. It is a family tradition.

Delphi—(What is the date?)—Arrived at last after a tedious journey. The inn is very uncomfortable. This is too bad, as in the guide book (Odysseus') it is marked with a constellation of the Pleiades, which means very good. The wine tastes of tar. And the salt is a chemical compound called Σερεβος. I made a scene and asked for ordinary slaves' salt, and they hadn't got any.

Shall not stay at this inn again, and I shall warn others not to. It is called ΞΕΝΩΛΟΧΕΙΟΝ ΒΑΓΟΝΛΗ. Disappointed in the Temple (very late architecture) and still more in the Oracle. I suppose it thought I didn't pay enough. But because one happens to be a prince, I don't see why one should be robbed. Besides which. I am travelling incognito as Kyrios Ralli. But the priests bowed, and they all called me, "your Shiningness." The Oracle was quite absurd, and evidently in a very bad temper. It said I would kill my father and marry my mother. It only shows how absurd the whole thing is. I hate superstition, and oracles ought to be stopped by law. Gypsies on the roadside are put in gaol. Why should oracles be supported by the State? I shall write to the False Witness about it.

In the afternoon went to the theatre. Saw the tragedy of Adam and Eve, a historical drama, translated from the Hebrew. Very long. The part of the Archangel, danced by Thepsis, was very bad, and the man who danced Eve was too old; but the snake was good. Scenery fine, especially the tree (which had real leaves).

Daulis, Tuesday—Arrived this morning. Very disappointing; the famous Daulian nightingale is not singing this spring. Just my luck. Rather an amazing incident happened yesterday on the way. My chariot was run into by a stranger. He was on the wrong side of the road, and, of course, entirely in the wrong. Also, his charioteer was not sober. We shouted, and we gave them ample room, and time, but he ran straight into us and his chariot was upset. The owner and charioteer were both taken to the Æsculapian Home, which is under the management of the Red Serpent. The doctor said it was serious. We did all we could, but had to go on, as I was due at Daulis to-day.

Thebes, a year later—Staying with Queen Jocasta, a charming widow. All very comfortable. Everybody is concerned about the Sphinx, who is really causing great annoyance, asking impertinent riddles, and playing dangerous practical jokes on people who can't answer. They want me to go. Very tiresome, as I never could answer a riddle; but it's difficult to refuse.

Wednesday—Saw the Sphinx. Guessed the riddle first shot. It asked what was that which runs on two legs, has feathers and a beak, and barks like a dog. I said "pheasant," and I added, "You put that in about the barking to make it more difficult." The Sphinx was very angry and went off in a huff, for good.

Thursday—As a reward for getting rid of the Sphinx I am allowed to marry the Queen; we are engaged. Everybody thinks it an excellent thing. She is a little older than I am; but I don't think that matters.

(Ten years later)

Thebes—Rather a severe epidemic of plague. They say it is not bubonic, however. In fact, it is what they call plagueen. Still, there are a great many deaths.

Thebes, a week later—The plague increasing. Have sent for Tiresias to find out what it comes from.

Tuesday—Tiresias arrived. Very cross and guarded. Don't believe he knows anything about it. Doesn't want to commit himself. He loves making mysteries.

Saturday—Insisted on Tiresias speaking out. Regret having done so now. He flew into a passion, and threatened the whole court with "exposure" and "revelations." That's the last thing we want now.

Monday—Had it all out with Tiresias. He told the most absurd cock and bull story. Utterly preposterous, but very disagreeable even to have such things hinted. Said nothing to Jocasta, as yet. Luckily, there are no proofs. Tiresias has raked up an old shepherd, who is ready to swear I am not the son of the King of Corinth, but the son of Laius, King of Thebes, and of Jocasta (my wife!); and that Laius was the man I accidentally killed years ago on the road to Daulis!

Tiresias says this is the sole cause of the plague, which is getting worse. They now say it is Asiatic.

Thursday—I interviewed and cross-examined the shepherd in the presence of Tiresias. There seems to be no doubt whatsoever about the facts. But I cannot see that any good can be done now, after all these years, by making a public scandal. It is, after all, a family matter. Tiresias says the plague will not stop unless the whole truth is published. Very awkward. Don't know how to break it to Jocasta.

Friday (dictated)—Jocasta overheard me discussing the matter with Tiresias and jumped, rashly, to conclusions. She had hysterics, and, losing all self-control, seriously injured both my eyes with a pin. I may very likely be blind for life. She was very sorry afterwards, and is now laid up. I and the children leave for Colonnus to-morrow, and it is settled that I am to abdicate in favour of Creon on the plea of ill-health and overwork. The children have been told nothing; but Antigone, who is far too precocious, alluded to Jocasta as grand-mamma. The matter will be hushed up as far as possible.

Citium Colonnus, two months later—The air here is delicious. Must say the change is doing me good.

CHAPTER XIII

FROM THE DIARY OF WILLIAM THE CONQUEROR

Rouen, 1066—Disquieting news from London. My friend, benefactor and relation, my brother Sovereign, Edward of England, has again had one of his attacks. It comes, I am sure, from not eating meat. Were anything to happen to him, I should be obliged to go over to London at once and settle as to the carrying on of the Government with Harold. Nothing could be more inconvenient at the present moment. Have the utmost confidence in Harold; but I fear the influence of the English nobility. I like the English; but they are not to be trusted in foreign politics. They are naturally perfidious, and they don't know it. They think they are more virtuous than other people; or rather that they are exempted from the faults and the vices which are common to us all. The European situation seems unsatisfactory.

Among other things Father Anselm writes that a certain party among the Englishwomen want to be admitted to the Witenagemot. The majority of the women are against it. The agitators sent a deputation to Westminster, but the King said it would not be according to the precedents to receive them. They were so annoyed at this that they made a dastardly attack on the beautiful old Druid Temple of Stonehenge, almost completely destroying it. F. Anselm says only a few blocks of stone are left, and that the place is unrecognisable.

The ringleaders were taken and claimed the ordeal by fire and the matter was referred to the Archbishop of Canterbury, who said that it was not a matter to be dealt with by ordeal. (Quite right!) He put the case into the hands of a select body of matrons, chosen from all classes. These decided that the offenders should be publicly whipped by women and sent home. This was done, much to the satisfaction of everybody.

Rouen—Heard Mass and went out hunting. Excellent sport. Shot a fox and six thrushes. Had thrush-pie for dinner. Find it difficult to get on horse-back without aid.

Rouen—Received a letter from the Pope. He says that should anything happen to King Edward—he is, of course, far from suggesting such a thing, but one must take everything into consideration—I must be very firm about claiming the succession. H.H. says that although, of course, it would be indelicate for him to raise the question just now, he knows it is the King's wish that I should succeed him. He seems to think Harold may give trouble. But Harold is bound to me by oath. Also I saved his life.

Rouen—Took William out hunting. His red hair frightens the ducks. Have told him over and over again to get a close-fitting green cap. The boys are always quarrelling. I don't know what is to be done with them. Robert broke his new battle-axe yesterday in a fit of passion.

My only consolation is that Henry is really making some progress with his tutor. He last learnt the alphabet as far as the letter F.

Rouen—A fisherman arrived last night from Southampton with the news that King Edward is dead. The news, he said, was confirmed by the appearance of a strange star with a tail to it in the sky. I have questioned the courier and gathered he had only got the news at second-hand. The rumour is probably baseless.

Rouen—The regular courier did not arrive this evening. The bag was brought by an Englishman. The official bulletin states that the King is slightly indisposed owing to a feverish cold, which he caught while inspecting the newly-raised body of archers, in the New Forest. A private letter from the archbishop tells me, in strict confidence, that the King's illness is more dangerous than people think. The children again quarrelled to-day. Matilda, as usual, took Henry's part, and said I was to blame. These domestic worries are very trying at such a critical moment. As a matter of fact, Henry teases his elder brothers, and boasts to them of his superior scholarship; they retaliate, naturally enough, by cuffing the boy, who complains at once to his mother. Since Henry has mastered the rudiments of the alphabet, his conceit has been quite beyond bounds. Of course, I admit it is clever of him. He is a clever boy. There is no doubt about that, but he shouldn't take advantage of it.

Rouen—Again the regular courier has not arrived. The bag again brought by an Englishman. According to a bulletin the King is going on well. Received a very friendly note from Harold, putting Pevensey Castle at my disposal, should I visit England in the autumn—and suggesting sport in the New Forest.

Rouen—Messenger arrived direct from London, via Newhaven. He says the King died last week, and that Harold has proclaimed himself King. Matilda said this would happen from the first. I think there can be no doubt that the news is authentic. The messenger, who is an old servant of mine, is thoroughly to be trusted. He saw the King's body lying in state. This explains why the regular messengers have not arrived. Harold had them stopped at the coast. This, in itself, is an unfriendly act. Matilda says I must invade England at once. Think she is right. But wish war could be avoided. Have written to the Pope asking for his moral support. Invasion a risky thing. Discussed the matter with General Bertram, who is an excellent strategist. He says he can devise fifty ways of landing troops in England, but not one way of getting them out again. That is just it. Supposing we are cut off? The English army is said to be very good indeed.

Rouen—Invasion of England settled. Must say have great misgivings on the subject. If we fail, the King of France is certain to attack us here. Matilda, however, won't hear of any other course being taken. Have privately sent a message to Harold proposing that we should settle the matter in a friendly fashion—I offer him nearly all Wessex, Wales and Scotland and the North—I taking the rest of the Kingdom, including London and Winchester. His situation is by no means entirely enviable. His brothers are certain to fight him in the North, and the King of Norway may also give trouble.

Rouen—Received letter from the Pope entirely approving of invasion. Sends me back banner, blessed. Received a letter from Harold also. Very insulting. Answers vaguely and commits himself to nothing. Ignores the past. Seems to forget I saved him from shipwreck and that he solemnly swore to support my claims. Seems also to forget that I am the lawful heir to the English throne. The crowning insult is that he addressed the letter to Duke William the Bastard.

Have ordered mobilisation to take place at once. The war is popular. Matilda and I were loudly cheered when we drove through the market place this afternoon. War will be a good occupation for the boys. Robert wants to stop here as Regent. Do not think this wise.

Hastings—Very disagreeable crossing. Took medicine recommended by Matilda (nettle leaves and milk and cinnamon), but did no good. Harold apparently defeated his brother in the North. Expect to fight to-morrow. Temper of the troops good. Terrain favourable, but cannot help feeling anxious.

London—Everything sadly in need of thorough reorganisation. Have resolved to carry out following initial reforms at once:—

1. Everybody to put out their lights by 8. Bell to ring for the purpose. The people here sit up too late, drinking. Most dangerous.

2. Enroll everybody in a book. Make it compulsory for the leeches to attend the poor, and dock serfs of a part of their wage, in order to create a fund for paying the leeches. (Think this rather neat.)

Shall tolerate no nonsense from the women. Matilda agrees that their complaints are ridiculous.

News from Normandy disquieting. Robert seems to be taking too much upon himself. Something must be done.

Going next week to New Forest to hunt. Very fine wild pony hunting there.

CHAPTER XIV

FROM THE DIARY OF MARY, MRS JOHN MILTON (née POWELL)

Aldersgate Street, July 1, 1643—House-keeping not quite such fun as I thought it would be. John is very particular. He cannot eat mutton, or any kind of hashed meat. He compares the cooking here unfavourably with that of Italy. He says the boys in the school are very naughty and that, during the Latin lesson this morning, one boy, called Jones minor, put a pin on his chair, just before he sat down on it. I couldn't help laughing; and this made John cross. He is thinking of writing a poem about King Arthur (sic) and the burnt cakes.

July 6—John has begun his poem. He makes it up during meals, which makes him forget to eat, and makes the meal very gloomy; he writes it down afterwards. He read me a long piece of it last night; but as it is in Latin I did not understand very much of it.

July 7—John and I quarrelled. It was about Jones minor. John announced the news of a reported rebel success during the boys' Greek lesson, and told the boys to give three cheers for the rebel army, which, of course, they all did, as they would never dare to disobey, except one brave hero, I call him, called Jones minor (the son of a tinker, bless him!), who called out as loud as he could: "Long live King Charles and death to all traitors!" John told him to repeat what he had said, and he did, and John caned him. I think this was very wrong on John's part, because, of course, the rebels are traitors. I took the part of the boy, and this made John angry. Then I said: "Of course, if all loyalists are so wicked, why did you marry me? My father is loyal and I am heart and soul for the King and the Church." John said that women's politics didn't count; but that the young must be taught discipline; that he was tolerant of all sincere opinion, however much he disagreed with it; but that the boy had merely wished to be insolent, by flying in the face of public opinion and the will of the school, which was the will of the people, and therefore the will of God, merely to gain a cheap notoriety. I said that probably all the boys felt the same, but didn't dare say so, as they knew that he, John, was on the other side. John said there are only seven "malignants" in the school. He said the boys were very angry with Jones minor and kicked him. I said they were a set of cowards. John said did I mean he was a coward, and quoted Greek. I said I didn't understand Greek and didn't want to. "That comes from your false education," said John; "your parents deserve the severest blame." I said that if he said anything against my parents, I would leave the house, and that my father knew Latin as well as he did. John said I was exaggerating. I said that I had often heard Papa say that John's Latin verses were poor. John said when his epick on King Alfred and the Lady of the Lake would be published, we should see who knew how to write Latin. I said: "Who?" John said I was flighty and ignorant. I said I might be ignorant, but at least I wasn't a rebel. John said I was too young to understand these things, and that, considering my bringing up, I was right to hold the opinions I did. When I was older I would see that they were false. Then I cried.

July 6—We made up our quarrel. John was ashamed of himself, and very dear, and said he regretted that he had used such vehement language. I forgave him at once.

July 9—We had some friends to dinner. Before we sat down, John said: "We will not mention politicks, as we might not all agree and that would mar the harmony of the symposium." But towards the end of dinner, I drank the King's health, quite unwittingly and from force of habit, forgetting—

This made John angry and led to a discussion, some of our guests taking the King's part and others saying that he was quite wrong. The men became very excited, and a young student, called Wyatt, whom John had invited because he is very musical and cultivated, threw a glass of wine in the face of Mr Lely, the wine-merchant, who is a violent rebel, and this broke up the party. John said that all "malignants" were the same; and that they none of them had any manners; that they were a set of roystering, nose-slitting, dissolute debauchees. When I thought of my dear father, and my dear brothers, this made me very angry; but I thought it best to say nothing at the time, as John was already annoyed and excited.

July 10—John says he can't make up his mind whether to write his epick poem in Latin or in Hebrew. I asked him whether he couldn't write it in English. He told me not to be irrelevant. The city is very dreary. John disapproves of places of public amusement. He is at the school all day; and in the evening he is busy thinking over his poem. Being married is not such fun as I thought it would be, and John is quite different from what he was when he courted me in the country. Sometimes I don't think he notices that I am there at all. I wish I were in the country.

July 11—John was in good temper to-day, because a scholar came here yesterday who said he wrote Italian very well. He asked me for my advice about his epick poem—which I thought was the best subject for an epick, King Arthur and the Cakes or the story of Adam and Eve. This made me feel inclined to laugh very much. Fancy writing a poem on the story of Adam and Eve! Everybody knows it! But I didn't laugh out loud, so as not to hurt his feelings, and I said "Adam and Eve," because I felt, somehow, that he wanted me to say that. He was so pleased, and said that I had an extraordinarily good judgment, when I chose. We had some cowslip wine for dinner which I brought from the country with me. John drank my health in Latin, which was a great favour, as he never says grace in Latin, because he says it's Popish.

July 14—John is thinking of not writing an epick poem after all, at least not yet, but a history of the world instead. He says it has never been properly written yet.

July 15—John has settled to translating the Bible into Latin verse. I am afraid I annoyed him; because when he told me this, I said I had always heard Papa say that the Bible was written in Latin. He said I oughtn't to talk about things which I didn't understand.

July 28—I am altogether put about. There are two Irish boys in the school; one is called Kelley and comes from the North, and the other is called O'Sullivan and comes from the South. They had a quarrel about politicks and O'Sullivan called Kelley a rebel, a heretick, a traitor to his country, a renegade, a coward and a bastard; and Kelley said that O'Sullivan was an idolater and a foreigner, and ended up by saying he hoped he would go and meet the Pope.

"Do you mean to insult the Pope before me?" said O'Sullivan.

"Yes," said Kelley, "to hell with your Pope."

I could hear and see all this from my window, as the boys were talking in the yard.

Kelley then shouted, "To hell with the Pope!" as loud as he could three times, and O'Sullivan turned quite white with rage, but he only laughed and said quite slowly:

"Your father turned traitor for money, just like Judas." Then the boys flew at each other and began to fight; and at that moment John, who was thinking over his epick poem in the dining-room, rushed out and stopped them. Then he sent for both the boys and asked them what it was all about, but they both refused to say a word. Then John sent for the whole school, and said that unless some boy told him exactly what had happened, he would stop all half-holidays for a month. So Pyke, a boy who had been there, told the whole story. John caned both O'Sullivan and Kelley for using strong language.

In the evening Mr Pye came to dinner, from Oxford. He teaches the Oxford boys physic or Greek philosophy; I forget which. But no sooner had we sat down to dinner than he began to abuse the rebels, and John, who was already cross, said that he did not suppose Mr Pye meant to defend the King. Mr Pye said he had always supposed that that was a duty every true-born Englishman took for granted; and John became very angry. I never heard anybody use such dreadful language. He said the King was a double-faced, lying monkey, full of Popish anticks, a wolf disguised as a jackass, a son of Belial, a double-tongued, double-faced, clay-footed, scarlet Ahithophel, and Mr Pye was so shocked that he got up and went away. I said that people who insulted the King were rebels, however clever they might be, and that it was dreadful to use such language; and when I thought of his beating those two little boys this morning for using not half such strong language it made me quite mad. John said that I was illogical. I said I wouldn't hear any more bad language; and I ran upstairs and locked myself in my room.

August 1, Oxfordshire—I have come home. I couldn't bear it. John was too unjust. Whenever I think of those two Irish boys and of John's language at dinner, my blood boils. Went out riding this morning with the boys. Papa says the war news is better, and that the rebels will soon be brought to heel.

CHAPTER XV

FROM THE DIARY OF MARK ANTONY

Alexandria (undated)—The reception went off very well. The Queen came to meet me by water in her State barge. She is different from what I remember her long ago, when I caught a glimpse of her in Rome. Then she was rather a colourless young girl, who had the reputation of being very well read, and rather affected. But now ... when you look at her face and you look away, you see green from the flash, as though you had been staring at the sun. She dazzles and blinds you. I received her in the market place. Her curtsey was a miracle of grace. She was very civil and dignified. After I had received her in the market place, I went to her palace. Such is the etiquette. I invited her to supper; but she insisted on my being her guest. I accepted. Supper in her palace. Semi-state, as the court is in mourning for Archilaus, the King of Cappadocia's eldest son, the Queen's first cousin. The ladies in waiting wore gold ornaments only. One of them, Charmian, pretty. The Queen, dropping all formality, was very lively and excellent company. The supper was good (the boars well roasted) and not so stiff as those kind of entertainments are as a rule.

After supper we had music and some dancing. Egyptian Bacchanals, who did a modern thing called Ariadne in Naxos. Very noisy and not much tune in it; but the dancing good, although hardly up to the Scythian standard.

Mardian, who has a fine contralto voice (he has been admirably trained), sang a piece from a ballet on the siege of Troy arranged by Æschylus. Very good. I like those old-fashioned things much better. They say it's conventional and out of date; but I don't care. The Queen told me in confidence that she quite agreed with me, but that even classical music bored her, so after we had listened to one or two odes, she asked Mardian to sing something light, some songs in dialect, which he did. Very funny, especially the one which begins:

"As I was going to Brindisi, upon a summer's day."

We made him sing that one twice. The Greeks know how to be witty without even being in the least vulgar.

Alexandria, three weeks later—Time has passed very quickly. Everybody is being so kind, and the Queen has taken immense pains to make everything a success. Most amusing improvised banquet in fancy dress last night. The Queen disguised as a fish-wife. She made me dress up, too. I put on a Persian private soldier's uniform. After supper we went into the town, in our disguises. Nobody recognised us, and we had the greatest fun. I threw pieces of orange-peel on the pavement. It was too comic to see the old men trip up over them. Then we went into a tavern on the first floor, and ate oysters. The Queen heated some coppers at the fire, and, after putting them on a plate with a pair of pincers, threw them out of the window. It was quite extraordinarily funny to see the beggars pick them up and then drop them with a howl! I don't think I ever laughed so much! The Queen has a royal sense of humour. And I who thought beforehand she was a blue-stocking! It shows how mistaken one can be.

Alexandria—Time seems to fly. No news from Rome. Wish the Queen would not be quite so ostentatiously lavish on my account. Eight wild boars for breakfast is too much. And the other night at supper she wasted an immense pearl in drinking my health in vinegar. This kind of thing makes people talk. She is wonderfully witty. She can mimic exactly the noises of a farmyard. Nothing seems to tire her, either. She will sit up all night and be ready early the next morning to go out fishing, sailing or anything else. She must have a constitution of steel. Wonderful woman!

Alexandria, later—News from Rome. Fulvia is dead: must go at once.

Rome, a month later—Engaged to be married to Octavia, Cæsar's sister, a widow. Purely a political alliance. Cleopatra is sure to understand the necessity of this. It is a great comfort to think that she is reasonable and has a real grip of the political situation.

Athens, a month later—Political situation grows more and more complicated. Octavia is very dutiful and most anxious to please. Do not think the climate here agreeable. The wind is very sharp and the nights are bitterly cold. Never did care for Athens.

Think that if I went to Egypt for a few days I could (a) benefit by change of air, (b) arrange matters with the Eastern Kings. Cæsar and Lepidus are trying to do me in the eye.

Athens, a day later—Octavia has very kindly offered to go to Rome, so as to act as a go-between between myself and Cæsar. She says she is quite certain it is all only a misunderstanding and that she can arrange matters. Thought it best not to mention possibility of Egyptian trip, as I may not go, after all.

Alexandria—Back here once more after all. Doctors all said change of air was essential, and that the climate of Athens was the very worst possible for me, just at this time. They said I should certainly have a nervous breakdown if I stayed on much longer. Besides which, it was absolutely necessary for me to be on the spot, to settle the Eastern Question. It is now fortunately settled. Cleopatra delighted to see me; but most reasonable. Quite understood everything. She did not say a word about Octavia. Reception in Alexandria magnificent. Ovation terrific. Shows how right I was to come back. Settled to proclaim Cleopatra Queen of Egypt, Lower Syria, Cyprus and Lydia. Everybody agrees that this is only fair.

Alexandria—Public proclamation in the market place. Settled to keep Media, Parthia and Armenia in the family, so divided them among the children. Ceremony went off splendidly. Cleopatra appeared as the

Goddess Isis. This was much appreciated, as it showed the people she really is national. The cheering was terrific.

Staying with us at present are the King of Libya, the King of Cappadocia, the King of Paphlagonia, the King of Thrace, the King of Arabia, the King of Pont, the King of Jewry, the King of Comagena, the King of Mede, and the King of Lycaonia. Question of precedence a little awkward. Herod, the King of Jewry, claimed precedence over all the other Kings on the grounds of antiquity and lineage. The King of Mede contested the claim, and the King of Arabia said that he was the oldest in years. There is no doubt about this, as he is 99. It was obvious the first place belonged to him. Question very neatly settled by Cleopatra. That they should rank according to the number of years they have reigned. She said this was the immemorial Egyptian custom, established by the Pharaohs and written out very carefully on a step of the great Pyramid. Everybody satisfied. King of Arabia takes precedence, but not on account of his age. Herod still a little touchy, but had to give in.

Played billiards with Cleopatra. Gave her 20. Won with difficulty. Cæsar is certain to make war on us. Have written to Octavia explaining everything fully.

In Camp near Actium—Nothing doing. One wonders whether Cæsar means to fight after all. The mosquitoes are very annoying. Impossible to get any milk.

In Camp near Actium, later—Cleopatra has arrived. She is used to camp life and does not mind roughing it. Everybody advises me to fight on land and not by sea, but Cleopatra and myself think we ought to fight by sea. Cæsar has taken Toryne. We have sixty sail. The thing is obvious; but soldiers are always prejudiced. Enobarbus worrying me to death to fight on land.

Cleopatra won't hear of it, and I am quite certain she is right. A woman's instinct in matters of strategy and tactics are infallible; and then—what a woman!

Alexandria, later—Very glad to be home again. Cleopatra was perfectly right to retreat. Played billiards. Gave Cleopatra 25. She beat me. She will soon be able to give me something. She is a surprising woman. Last night the Greek envoy dined. Too clever for me, but Cleopatra floored him over Anaxagoras. Wonderful woman! She sang, or rather hummed, in the evening a little Greek song, the burden of which is

Ἐγὼ δὲ μόνα καθεύδω.

I cannot get the tune out of my head.

CHAPTER XVI

FROM THE DIARY OF IVAN THE TERRIBLE

Moscow, September 1, 1560—I drove to the village of O——, 24 versts. On one side of the river is the village, with its church, on the other a lonely windmill. The landscape flat and brown, the nearer houses and the distant trees sharp in the clear autumn air. The windmill is maimed; it has lost one of its wings. It is like my soul. My soul is a broken windmill which is rusty, stiff, and maimed; it groans and creaks before the winds of God, but it no longer turns; and no longer, cheerfully grumbling as of yore, it performs its daily task and grinds the useful corn. The only spots of colour in the landscape were the blue cupolas of the church; a blue and red shirt hanging up to dry on an apple-tree near a wooden hut, and the kerchiefs of the women who were washing linen in the river. A soldier talked to the women, and laughed with them. I would that I could laugh like that with men and women. I can only laugh alone and bitterly. I had never been there before. But when lazily, a cock crew, and a little boy made music on a wooden pipe, and a long cart laden with sacks creaked by, the driver walking by its side, I knew that I had seen all this before, not something like unto it, but this very thing, that same windmill, that same creaking cart, that same little boy playing that very tune on that very pipe.

It was a mournful tune, and it said to my soul, "Why art thou so dusty and rusty, O my soul, why art thou sorrowful? Crusted with suspicion; uneasy and fearful, prompt to wrath and slow to trust, inhospitable towards hope, and a stranger to gladness?"

The world is a peep-show, and I have satisfied my expectation. I am weary of the sights of the fair, and the mirth of the crowd to me is meaningless. The bells, and the tambourines, and the toy trumpets, the grating of the strings, and the banging of the drum jar upon me. Like a child, who has spent a whole day in frolic and whose little strength is utterly exhausted, I desire to go home and to rest.

Rest, where is there any rest for thee, Ivan, Ivan the Restless? Everywhere have I sought for peace and found it nowhere, save in a cell, and on my knees, before the Image.

September 10—Why was I born to be a King?

Why was I cast, a frail and fearful infant, to that herd of ravenous wolves, those riotous nobles, that band of greedy, brutal, and ruthless villains who bled my beloved country and tore my inheritance into shreds? I think I know why I was sent thither. Out of the weakness came forth strength; a little boy was sent forth to slay the giant. I was sent to deliver the Russian people, to break the necks of the nobles, and to cast the tyrants from their stronghold. I was sent to take the part of the people, and they will never forget this or me; in years to come, ages after I am dead, mothers will sing their children to sleep with songs about the great Tsar of Moscow, Ivan the well-beloved, Ivan the people's friend, Ivan the father of the fatherless, the brother of the needy, the deliverer of the oppressed.

But the proud and the mighty, the rich and the wicked, shall hate me and vilify me, and blacken my name. I know you, ye vipers, and all your ways. I would that not one of you could escape me; but, like the hydra, you have a hundred heads, that grow again as fast as they are cut off. When I am gone, O vile and poisonous nobility, you will raise your insolent head once more, and trample again upon my beloved people.

Would that I could utterly uproot you from the holy soil of Russia, and cast you to perish like weeds into a bottomless pit.

October 1—I dreamed last night a fearful dream. I dreamed that I had done an abominable thing, and that I bore stains on my hands that the snows of the mountains and the waves of the sea could not wash out. I dreamed that all mankind shunned me, and that I wandered alone across the great plain till I came to the end of the world and the gates of Heaven. I knocked at the gates, but they were shut; and round me there was a multitude, and there arose from it a sound of angry voices, crying, "He has slain our fathers, and our brothers, and our mothers, by him our houses were burnt and our homes were laid waste, let him not enter"; and I knocked at the gate, and then there came a man with a mark on his brow, and he said, "This man has killed his son, let him not in." And I knew that man was Cain. And the howling of the voices grew louder, and the cries of hate surging round me deafened me. I knocked, and prayed, and cried, and wept, but the gate remained shut. And all at once I was left alone in the great plain deserted even by my enemies, and I shivered in the darkness and in the silence. Then, along the road, came a pilgrim, a poor man, begging for alms, and when he saw me, he knelt before me, and I said, "Wherefore dost thou kneel to me, who am deserted by God and man?" And he answered, "Is not sorrow a holy thing? Thou art the most sorrowful man in the whole world, for thou hast killed what was dearer to thee than life, and bitter is thy sorrow, and heavy is thy punishment." And the pilgrim kissed my hand, and the hot tears that he shed fell upon it.

And at that moment, far away I heard a noise as of gates turning on a great hinge, and I knew that the doors of Heaven were open.

Then I awoke, and I crept up the stairway way to my little son's bedroom. He lay sleeping peacefully. And I knelt down and thanked Heaven that the dream was but a dream; but when the sun rose in the morning, like a wave from out of infinity, apprehension rolled to my soul and settled on it. I am afraid, and I know not of what I am afraid.

February 13, 1570—Thanks to God Novgorod is no more. I have utterly destroyed its city and its people for its contumacy. So fare all the enemies of Russia and of Moscow.

CHAPTER XVII

FROM THE PRIVATE LOG OF CHRISTOPHER COLUMBUS

On Board the Santa Maria.

August 3, 1492, Friday—At five in the morning made the signal to weigh: but in less than half an hour the wind shifting to the southward and blowing fresh, I furled the topsails. The wind came in the afternoon to S. by W.; we weighed, but did not get far, the flood tide making against us.

August 4—Little wind, or calm, all day. Send-off very fine; but now that we have started wonder whether I have been wise after all. Wonder whether we shall reach Western India and China.

August 5—Took the meridian observation at midday; wind northerly with a great swell. Ship's company in good spirits: but the doctor says we have started on a wild goose chase.

August 8—Stood close in with the land. At noon the latitude by observation was 28 degrees 18 minutes. Stood in to a small bay to the southward of Teneriffe. Anchored with the stream anchor, and sent the boat for water. Went ashore with the astronomer and instruments. All the liberty men came on board the worse for liquor, which is, on the whole, fortunate, as we shall have no trouble in getting them to continue the voyage.

August 9—Several of the men confined with colds, and complain of pains in their bones. But from the careful attendance given them, doses of "Skulker's Mixture" being administered by the doctor all round, few continued in the sick list. The air very warm.

September 9—Thick fog. At five the officer informed me that we were near an iceberg. I ordered the ship to be kept N. by W. and hauled farther in. At noon I steered north, seeing nothing of the ice; soon after I was told that they saw the ice: I went upon deck and perceived something white upon the bow, and heard a noise like the booming of surf. I hauled down the studding sails and hailed the Niña and the Pinta: I desired that they would keep close to us, the fog being so thick, and have everybody up ready to follow our motions instantaneously, determining to stand under such sail as should enable us to keep the ships under command, and not risk parting company. Soon afterwards, we saw something on the bow, which from the appearance we took to be islands, and thought we had not stood far enough out. The ship's company raised a cheer. I hauled up immediately to the N.N.W., and was soon undeceived, finding it to be a moderate-sized sea serpent, which we could not clear upon that tack; we tacked immediately, but the wind and sea both setting directly upon it, we neared it very fast, and were within a little more than a cable's length of the animal whilst in stays.

The doctor, who has always scoffed at the idea of the sea serpent, which, he said, was a travellers' tale (adding, sarcastically, and, I think, very inconsiderately, "like the western passage to China"), was silent all the evening.

Prefer this to his irritating reiteration of that silly Andalusian song:

And if we ever get back to Spain
We will never, never, never go to sea again,

which he is so fond of indulging in. Sea serpent of the ordinary kind, with a white ring round its neck and a tufted crest. Not so large as the Icelandic specimens. Expect to reach China in ten days' time, should the weather be favourable. Officers and ship's company in decidedly less good spirits since the foggy weather began. Sea serpent incident also caused a good deal of disappointment, the men being convinced we had reached the coast of China, although I had repeatedly explained that we could not possibly make that land for some time yet.

September 10—Lost the Niña and the Pinta twice in the night from the very thick fog. The situation of the men from the very fatiguing work made most minute precautions necessary. Double allowance of Manzanilla served round to-day.

September 11—No land in sight. Calm all day, with a great swell from the S.W., and the weather remarkably mild. Confess am disappointed; wonder whether there is such a country as China after all. Confess I have no satisfactory evidence for thinking so. But am concealing my anxiety, of course, from the officers and the doctor, who grow more and more sarcastic every day. He said at dinner yesterday that we might come home by the Nile, as we should certainly encounter its source in China. Want of taste. It is only too plain that both officers and ship's company are growing sceptical as to the practical results of our voyage. Wish the King and Queen of Spain had been a little less sanguine. We shall indeed look very foolish if we come back having accomplished nothing.

September 12—Ship's company distressingly sulky. If matters continue like this it will end in a mutiny. Have been obliged to fake the observations, measuring the ship's way so that the ship's company should remain in ignorance of the distances traversed, and think that they are much less than they are in reality.

This faking has been an easy task, since the log, being only a mean taken every hour and consequently liable to error from the variations in the force of the wind during the intervals, from which an arbitrary correction is made by the officer of the watch; as this allowance must from its nature be inaccurate, it is very easy to make it more inaccurate still, now, that is to say, that I have squared Roderigo.

September 13—Have made a startling and disagreeable discovery. There is something wrong or odd about the compass. The axis of the needle no longer coincides with the geographical meridian it occupies—but makes an angle. This matter must be investigated.

September 17—The ship's company discovered at dawn to-day the vagaries of the compass. Situation alarming. They at once said we must go home. Doctor and surgeon both say that they are not surprised. Roderigo has constructed an instrument, hanging by a universal joint on a triangular stand, adjusted so as to hang in a plane perpendicular to the horizon, by means of a plumb line, which is suspended on a pin above a divided circle. The length of the magnetic needle is 12 inches, and its axis is made of gold and copper.

Roderigo says he can now observe the variation. Most ingenious (if true).

September 18—Everybody expects to see land to-day. Why, I can't think. Sailors sometimes have strange superstitions.

September 25—We are now 475 leagues from the Canaries. No sign of land. I am quite convinced personally that there is no chance of our ever reaching land this voyage. I knew from the first the affair was hopeless. Feel certain we cannot be near China or India. Unfortunately, my conviction, which I have never expressed, is shared by the ship's company, who showed signs of positive mutiny to-day. Calmed them as best I could with soothing words and old sherry. Steered S. to W.

September 26—Steered W. No sign of anything. Wish we had never left Spain. The Alguazil disgracefully drunk again last night, and rude in his cups. Doctor sarcastic. Surgeon sea-sick. Ship's company mutinous. Have a bad headache. Never did like the sea. It never agreed with my liver.

October 7—I ordered the allowance of liquor to be altered, serving the ship's company one-fourth of their allowance in Manzanilla and the other three-fourths in brandy. One half of this allowance was served before dinner, and the other half in the evening. Result satisfactory.

Altered course W. to S.W.

October 10—Mutiny. Ship's company refuse to go on. Insist on returning to Spain. If I refuse they threaten to kill me; but I fear they will kill me if I consent. Otherwise the matter would be simple. Have asked for three days' respite. Roderigo saw a piece of driftwood and a small bird called a red-poll. Thinks we are not far from land. Too good to be true.

October 11—Saw a light on starboard bow, but am not quite certain that it wasn't a star.

October 12—Roderigo saw the land at two in the morning. The King promised a reward of 10,000 Maravedises to whoever saw land first. Clearly this reward is mine, as the light I saw on Thursday night was not a star. Explained this to Roderigo, who lost his temper, and said that if he didn't get the reward he would ton Mahommedan. The land is, of course, the coast of China. I always said it was somewhere about here.

Stood in to make the land. Anchored with the best bower in eleven fathoms, soft clay. Hoisted Spanish flag; took possession of the country, which seems to be India, and not China, after all. Call it West India or Hispaniola. Natives talk in a drawling sing-song, chew tobacco and gum, and drink Manzanilla and Vermouth mixed, icing the drink. This is a very gratifying mixture. It is called a Cola de gallo. They have a round game of cards with counters, called chips, in which you pretend to hold better cards than you do hold in reality. Played and lost. Natives very sharp.

CHAPTER XVIII

FROM THE DIARY OF THE MAN IN THE IRON MASK

Pignerol, August 21, 1669—Have at last, I think, attained my heart's desire. Arrived last night under the pseudonym of Eustache Danger. Found everything fairly satisfactory. That is to say, the King's promises to me with regard to the absolute solitude I crave have been carried out as far as was possible in the time. The prison is not finished, and this accounts for a fact which annoyed me not a little on my arrival. I found that the walls of my room were not of the thickness promised, so that, should any one be lodged next door to me, which Heaven forfend! he might have the bad taste to try and communicate with me by knocking on the wall. I wear a black velvet mask and the King solemnly promised me that if any officer were to dare to ask me who I was he would be instantly dismissed.

August 22, 1669—So far so good. Saint Mars, the Governor of the Prison, is certainly doing his best. But last night, when he brought me my dinner, he forgot himself and said, "Bon Soir, Monsieur." If he does this again he will have to be removed. I did not come here to be bothered with conversation.

August 25—I am enjoying myself immensely. The relief of waking up in the morning and of gradually becoming conscious that it will not be necessary—

(a) To dress in Court clothes.

(b) To go out hunting.

(c) To attend the King's lever, or still worse, his coucher.

(d) To play cards and lose.

(e) To listen to a play performed in a private house.

(f) To laugh at Madame—'s chaff.

(g) To make love to J—.

(h) To pretend to enjoy the beauties of nature.

(i) To hear and give opinions on Molière.

(j) To sit through the long, long dinner.

(k) To talk philosophy with Mademoiselle.

(l) To find fault with my servant for giving me the wrong stockings.

(m) To wait for hours in the crown of the Œil-de-Bœuf.

(n) To be taken to the window by the English Ambassador and asked if I think the Spaniards really mean business.

(o) To talk internal politics with Louvois.

(p) To listen to Le Nôtre's account of Lord Carlisle's new garden.

(q) To listen to Bossuet's sermon on Sunday.

(r) Not to annoy the Duchesse de La Vallière.

(s) To have to look as if I thought the King an amusing conversationalist.

(t) To say that a Bal Masqué is great fun.

(u) To go to the opera at the back of a box.

(v) To pretend I like Dutch pictures.

(w) To dance all night in a room like a monkey cage.

(x) To read the Gazette.

(y) To be civil to the German Ambassadress.

(z) To change my clothes three times a day.

That is my alphabet of negation. It is incomplete. Yet to write it and read it over and over again fills me with ecstasy.

March, 1670—A most annoying incident happened to-day. The upper tower, at the western angle of the Castle, is occupied by Fouquet and Lauzun. The King promised me solemnly that neither of them should be allowed to hold any communication with me. To-day one of Fouquet's servants entered my room and spoke to me, asking me whether I had anything of importance to communicate. I told him very sharply to go to the devil. If this happens again I shall ask to be moved to a quieter prison.

It is extraordinary that even in a place like this one cannot be free from the importunity and the impertinence of human curiosity.

April 3, 1670—As the days go on, I enjoy myself more and more. A cargo of books arrived yesterday from Paris, sent by the King, but Saint Mars had the good sense not to bring them to me. He merely notified the fact on a slip of paper, which he left on my plate. I scribbled a note to the effect that he could throw them to the bottom of the sea, or read them himself, or give them to Fouquet's servant. Books indeed! It is no longer, thank God, necessary for me to read books, or to have an opinion on them!

November 1, 1671—Lauzun has been sent here. The prison is getting far too crowded. It will soon be as bad as Versailles.

November 10—Lauzun is being very tiresome. He taps on my ceiling. I wrote a short note to Saint Mars that if this annoyance continued I should be constrained to leave his prison.

March 3, 1680—The situation was intolerable. Lauzun and Fouquet found some means of communication and they carried on interminable conversations. What they can have to talk about passes my understanding. I bore it patiently for some days. At last I complained to Saint Mars in writing, he took some steps and it appears that Fouquet has had an attack of apoplexy and died. I cannot endure the neighbourhood of Lauzun, and I have written to the King saying that unless I am transferred to a quieter dungeon I shall leave the prison.

April 8, 1680—Matters have been arranged satisfactorily, and I have been moved into the lower chamber of the Tour d'en bas. But the whole fortress is far too crowded. There are at least five prisoners in it. Also I found a tame mouse here, left I suppose by a former occupant. Had the nuisance removed at once. It is delicious to be safely in prison just now that the spring is beginning and to think that I shall not have to spend chilly evenings in wet gardens and to speak foolishly of the damp April weather.

January, 1681—Caused much annoyance by a tiresome Italian fellow prisoner called Mattioli, who, feigning either madness or illness, or both, caused a commotion in the prison, necessitating the arrival of doctors and priests. Kept awake by noise of bolts being drawn, and the opening and shutting of doors. Wrote to the King complaining of this which is a direct infringement of his promise. Asked to be moved to a quieter spot.

September 2,1681—Moved to the Fortress of Exiles. Prison said to be empty. Hope this will prove true.

October 10,1681—Saint Mars very nearly spoke to me to-day. He was evidently bursting with something he longed to communicate. However, I made such a gesture, that I think he felt the frown through my velvet mask and withdrew.

January 5, 1687—After months, and indeed years of peace, perfect peace, with loved ones far away, I have again been subjected to intolerable annoyance. Fouquet's valet fell ill, and Saint Mars informed me of the fact. I wrote to the King at once saying that either Saint Mars or I must go.

April 30, 1687—King has granted my request. Arrived at Sainte Marguerite in a chair with wheels covered with wax-cloth. I think I shall be quieter here. I have been promised that no other prisoner shall be lodged here at all, but the promises of Kings are as iridescent and as brittle as Venetian glass.

January, 1690—Alas! Alas! for the vanity of human wishes. Here I was perfectly contented, and, as I thought, quiet at last. Day followed day of perfect enjoyment, unmarred by conversation, undisturbed by study, unvexed by the elements, when the peace of my solitude is rudely shattered by the arrival of two Protestant ministers. It is true I am never to see them, but the mere fact of knowing that there are two Protestant ministers in the same building is enough to poison life!

June 1, 1698—More Protestant ministers have arrived, worse than the last. They sing hymns. I have written to the King asking him to transfer me to the Bastille at once. I always said that the Bastille was the only tolerable dwelling-place in France.

September 13, 1698—Arrived at the Bastille this afternoon. Lodged on the third floor of the Bertandière tower—the thickest tower. Really quiet.

September 19—A man hammered over my head at four o'clock this morning. It is intolerable. Shall I ever find a place where I can sleep from 4 to 8 a.m. without being disturbed? As it is, I might just as well be living in a fashionable inn.

CHAPTER XIX

FROM THE DIARY OF AN ENGLISH GOVERNESS RESIDING IN PARIS DURING THE FRENCH REVOLUTION

Paris, October 7, 1789—I arrived this afternoon after a rapid and satisfactory journey. To my amazement found that neither the Count nor the Countess were here to receive me. The Hotel was deserted save for the presence of an old servant, and his wife, who appears to be the cook of the household, and to combine with this office the duties of hall porter. As I have no command over even the elementary rudiments of the French language, and as the French never trouble to learn any language but their own, communication is a sorely difficult task and results in perpetual misunderstanding. Nevertheless, I succeeded in apprehending from the voluble expostulations and the superfluous gesticulation of the old servant, whose name appears to be Pierre, but whom I have decided to call Peter, that the family had left Paris. That they had departed but recently and in haste, my senses were able to inform me. All over the house were traces of disorder. Some but half-packed boxes had been left behind; cupboards were open, clothes were strewn on the floor, and everywhere traces of precipitate packing and sudden departure were manifest. I made as if I would depart also, but Peter made it plain by signs that I was expected to remain, and indeed he conducted me to my room, which is airy and commodious enough, and where, after partaking of a light supper, insufficient and badly cooked as all French meals, and accompanied by the sour "wine" of the country, I fell into a comfortable slumber.

October 10, 1789—I have now been here three days, and as yet I have received neither message, nor token, nor sign from the departed family, nor can I ascertain from Peter or his wife, the obtuse menials who are the sole occupants of this in some respects elegant mansion, whither they have gone: whether they are loitering in their country seat, or whether they have started on a longer peregrination. Paris is very full. The streets are ill-kept and ill-lit, a strange contrast to the blaze (at night) and tidiness (by day) of the London streets. It is a dingy city, and I think it must certainly be insanitary. The French understand no word of English, and if indeed one ventures to address them, all they reply is: "Rosbeef, plom pudding," a form of address which they consider facetious. The house is spacious enough, although inconveniently distant from the centre of the city, but it has the advantage of an extensive garden surrounded by high walls. As for myself, I am well cared for by Peter and his wife. She talks at me with great volubility, but I cannot understand a word of what she says. French is an unmusical language, very sharp and nasal, but not ill-suited to a backward people.

July 14, 1790—Went for a long walk in the city. The streets quiet and deserted. Peter and his wife went out for the day. She is very handy with her needle. I find altogether that the French are quite amenable to reason, if well treated. Of course, one cannot expect them to work like English people, but they are willing and do their best. It is unfortunate they do not speak English. Received last quarter's salary through the usual channel. No further views.

March 4, 1792—Went out in the evening with Peter and his wife. They took me to the Opera House, having apparently received tickets from a friend connected with theatrical affairs. Castor and Pollux was the name of the opera. The scenery was gorgeous, and the ballets very skilfully performed. The opera was given in French, so that I could not follow the words. Weather grey and dark. Boulevards as usual ill-lit; but crowded with people coming from the coffee-houses, the theatres and the out-of-door dining houses—all singing at the top of their voices. Returned home between nine and ten.

March 6, 1792—Again to the Opera House to hear the Alcestis of Gluck, and to see the celebrated Vestris dance in a ballet called Psyche. Scenery as usual gorgeous, singing nasal and most unpleasing.

August 13, 1792—Nothing worth recording. Spend most of the days in the garden. Weather hot. French people vulgar and loud in their holiday-making, partial also to fireworks, explosives, firing of guns, etc. I now make a point of-staying at home on Feast days and holidays, of which there are far too many.

Sunday, September 2, 1792—Read the morning service in the garden. Sultry.

January 21, 1793—Shops shut this morning, although it is Monday. No salary received for the last two quarters.

November 10, 1793—Sunday. Started out to walk along the river in spite of the damp weather. Streets very muddy. A great crowd of people near the Cathedral. Caught in the crowd and obliged to follow with the stream. Borne by the force of the crowd right into the church. Deeply shocked and disgusted at the display of Romish superstition. A live woman resembling a play actress throned near the altar, representing no doubt the Virgin Mary. Most reprehensible. Was obliged to assist at the mummery until the crowd departed. Think I have taken cold.

November 11, 1793—Have indeed taken cold in consequence of yesterday's outing. Remained indoors all day. Peter and his wife most obliging. They made me some hot negus flavoured with black currant, not unpalatable.

November 12,1793—Cold worse. Suffering from ague in the bones as well. Shall not get up to-morrow. Peter's wife spent much time in talking and screaming at me. Gathered from her rapid and unintelligible jargon that she wished me to see a doctor. Shook my head vehemently. Shall certainly not put myself in the hands of a French doctor. One never knows what foreigners may prescribe.

January 1, 1794—Came downstairs for the first time since I have been laid up. Made many good resolutions for the New Year. Among others to keep my journal more diligently.

May 30, 1794—Walked in the garden for the first time since my relapse. Peter's wife has nursed me with much care and tenderness. Still very weak.

July 30, 1794—First walk in the city since my long illness. Feel really better. Bought a lace kerchief.

October 1, 1794—The family, that is to say, the Countess and her two daughters, arrived unexpectedly in the night. Countess simple and kindly, can scarcely speak any English. Begin lessons to-morrow.

October 2, 1794—The eldest girl Amelia, aged seven, speaks English but has been shamefully ill-taught during her stay in England (for it appears the family have been in England!). She is sadly backward in spelling: but she has a fair accent and is evidently an intelligent child. Unfortunately, she has picked up many unseemly expressions. The Countess suggested my learning French, but I respectfully declined. Reading Pope's Essay on Man in the evenings. It is improving as well as elegant.

CHAPTER XX

FROM THE DIARY OF HAMLET, PRINCE OF DENMARK, DURING HIS STAY AT ENGLAND, WHITHER HE WAS SENT TO STUDY AT THE UNIVERSITY AT OXFORD, UNDER THE SPECIAL CARE OF POLONIUS

Balliol College, Monday—Read aloud my Essay on Equality to the Master. It began: "Treat all men as your equals, especially the rich." The Master commented on this sentence. He said, "Very ribald, Prince Hamlet, very ribald."

In training for the annual fencing match between the Universities of Oxford and Cambridge. Doing my utmost to reduce my flesh which is far too solid.

Tuesday—Went to Abingdon for the day. When I came back I found that havoc had been made of my rooms: both the virginals broken to pieces—all the furniture destroyed, and all my pictures including a signed portrait of Ophelia.

Have my suspicions as to who has done this. Shall first make certain and then retaliate terribly. In the meantime it will be politic to conceal my annoyance.

Friday—Dined last night with a society of Undergraduates who meet together in a Barn to discuss Falconry and French verse. Rhenish wine served in great quantities. Feigned drunkenness in order to discover who was guilty of taking liberties with my furniture. As I suspected, Rosencrantz and Guildenstern were the culprits. They as good as admitted it in their cups.

Intend to be revenged some day, and that royally.

Saturday—When we returned home from the barn last night, it was of course necessary for me to keep up the false semblance of intoxication with which I had started the evening.

This I did by improvising and singing quaint rhymeless couplets as we strutted across the Quadrangle of the College. It so chanced that we encountered the Dean, who addressed me. I answered, keeping up the part: "Buzz. Buzz."

Monday—A College meeting was held this morning and I was summoned to appear on the charges:—

(a) Of having been intoxicated.

(b) Of having insulted the Dean.

(c) Of having persuaded and finally compelled the younger members of the College to drink more than was good for them.

To which I replied (a) that seeing that I was in strict training it was obvious that the charge of intoxication was unfounded; (b) that so far from insulting the Dean, I had addressed him in Danish, and that familiar as I knew him to be with all the languages of Europe and especially the Scandinavian tongues, he had probably not realized to the full the exact shade of deference, respect, and awe which the expression I used implied; (c) that as far as the charge of corrupting the young was concerned, I was not ashamed to stand in the same dock with Socrates, and I would cheerfully, if the College authorities and my Royal parents thought fit, share the doom of my august master. Finally I reminded the noble and learned assembly that were I to be expelled, even temporarily, from the College I should be unable (a) to represent the Alma Mater with the rapier against the University of Cambridge, who had a powerful champion of the noble art in Laertes, a fellow-countryman of mine; and (b) I should not be able to row in the College boat. I concluded by saying that certain as I was that my royal parents would endorse any decision which should be arrived at by the Master and his Colleagues, I was convinced that were I to be sent down from the College, my royal father, in order that my studies might not be interrupted, would immediately send me to Cambridge.

The net result of all this is that I am admonished.

Later in the Day I received a note from the Dean asking me to dine with him next Thursday.

Sunday—Breakfasted with the Master to meet the Poet Laureate, the Archbishop of York, the Lord Chancellor, the French ambassador, and Quattrovalli, a celebrated Italian juggler. The poet laureate read out an Ode he had just composed on the King's sixth marriage. Very poor.

Monday—Took part in the debate held by the College Debating Society. The subject being whether Homer's Epics were written by Homer or by a Committee of Athenian Dons.

Took what seemed to the audience a paradoxical view that they were written by Homer.

Tuesday—Gave a small dinner party in my rooms. Horatio and a few others. Again compelled to feign intoxication, so as not to mar the harmony of the evening. Burnt a small organ, and rather a complicated printing press, belonging to a German undergraduate named Faustus, in the Quadrangle.

Wednesday—The master commenting on last night's bonfire said he thought it was not humorous, and fined us heavily. Have as yet found no opportunity of revenging myself on Rosencrantz and Guildenstern.

Thursday—Coached by Polonius for two hours in Scottish history. Very tedious. In the afternoon went on the river in my boat the "Ophelia." Faustus has been sent down for trying to raise the Devil in the precincts of the College. It appears this is strictly against the rules. His excuse was that he had always understood that the College authorities disbelieved in a personal devil. To which the Dean replied: "We are all bound to believe in the Devil in a spiritual sense, Mr Faustus." And Faustus imprudently asked in what other sense you could believe in him.

Friday—Must really settle this business of Rosencrantz and Guildenstern soon. It is beginning to prey upon my mind. They are quite insufferable. Have lost one stone since the term began, which is satisfactory. Fencing match is to take place next week, here.

Saturday—The man who has the rooms opposite mine is a Spaniard. A nobleman very cultivated and amiable. His name is Quixote. Consulted him last night as to what to do about Rosencrantz and Guildenstern. Quixote said it was entirely a point of honour. That if I were certain they were guilty, and certain likewise that they had purposely insulted me, I should challenge them each, separately, to personal combat, with sword and rapier. I pointed out, however, that whereas I was a champion swordsman, and indeed had been chosen to represent the University, they had no skill at all. Moreover, I considered that to challenge them to fight would be doing them too much honour. Quixote said I must indubitably, take action of some kind, or else I would incur the suspicion of cowardice. At that moment—we were talking by the open casement—I saw in the darkness, walking stealthily along the wall a man whom I took to be Guildenstern. Seizing a bottle of white wine from Xeres with which Quixote had entertained me, I flung it out of the window on to the head of the skulker, but alas! it was not Guildenstern but the Dean himself!

Monday—Again appeared before a College meeting. Accused of having wantonly wounded, and almost murdered the Dean. Protested my innocence in vain. It was further suggested I was intoxicated. Lost my temper, which was a mistake, and called the Dean a villain, losing control over my epithets.

Sent down for the rest of the term. Polonius is very angry. He has written to my father suggesting that I should not go back to Oxford, nor seek to enter Cambridge either, but go to Wittenberg instead. Owing to my abrupt departure the fencing match with Laertes will not come oft. No matter, a day will come, when maybe I shall be revenged on Rosencrantz and Guildenstern. We go to London to-day.

MAURICE BARING – A CONCISE BIBLIOGRAPHY

The Black Prince and Other Poems (1903)
With the Russians in Manchuria (1905)
Forget-me-Not and Lily of the Valley (1905)
Sonnets and Short Poems (1906)
Thoughts on Art and Life (1906)
Russian Essays and Stories (1908)
Orpheus in Mayfair and Other Stories (1909) Short stories

Dead Letters (1910) Satirical collection
The Glass Mender and Other Stories (1910)
The Russian People (1911)
Letters from the Near East (1913)
Lost Diaries (1913) Fictional extracts from diaries of notable people
The Mainsprings of Russia (1914)
Round the World in any Number of Days (1919)
Flying Corps Headquarters 1914-1918 (1920)
Passing By (1921) Novel
The Puppet Show of Memory (1922) Autobiography
Overlooked (1922) Short story
Poems 1914-1919 (1923)
C (1924) Novel
Punch and Judy and Other Essays (1924)
Half a Minute's Silence and Other Stories (1925)
Cat's Cradle (1925) Novel
Daphne Adeane (1926) Novel
Tinker's Leave (1927) Novel
Comfortless Memory (1928) Novel
The Coat Without Seam (1929) Novel
Robert Peckham (1930) historical Novel
In My End is My Beginning (1931) Biographical novel about Mary Stuart
Friday's Business (1932) Novel
Lost Lectures (1932) Imaginary lectures
The Lonely Lady of Dulwich (1934) Novella
Darby and Joan (1935) Novel
Have You Anything to Declare? (1936) Collection of notes and quotes
Collected Poems (1937) Poetry
Maurice Baring: A Postscript by Laura Lovat with Some Letters and Verse (1947)
Dear Animated Bust: Letters to Lady Juliet Duff, France 1915-1918
The Oxford Book Of Russian Verse (1924) Editor